For Lauren,
    after your stay in Ireland
June 11-21, 1995.
Dublin. Clonskeagh. Bray. Lahinch. Ennis.
Galway. Howth.

        love Paul.

IRELAND IN POETRY

IRELAND IN POETRY

WITH
PAINTINGS,
DRAWINGS,
PHOTOGRAPHS,
AND
OTHER
WORKS OF ART

EDITED BY CHARLES SULLIVAN

HARRY N. ABRAMS, INC., PUBLISHERS, NEW YORK

THIS BOOK IS DEDICATED TO
MY SON, CHARLES,
MY DAUGHTER-IN-LAW, MICHELLE,
AND MY GRANDSON,
FRANK HANAFEE SULLIVAN,
BUILDERS OF THE FUTURE

EDITOR:
MARGARET BLYTHE RENNOLDS

DESIGNER:
CAROL ANN ROBSON

RIGHTS AND REPRODUCTIONS:
JOHN K. CROWLEY, UTA HOFFMANN, AND MAXWELL SILVERMAN

LIBRARY OF CONGRESS CATALOGING-IN-PUBLICATION DATA

Ireland in poetry: with paintings, drawings, photographs, and other
works of art/edited by Charles Sullivan.
p.   cm.
ISBN 0–8109–3453–1
1. Ireland—Poetry. 2. English poetry—Irish authors. 3. English
poetry—Translations from Irish. 4. Irish poetry—Translations into
English. 5. Ireland in art. I. Sullivan, Charles, 1933–
PR8851.I65   1990
821.008′032415—dc20   90–205
CIP

Quality printing and binding by Toppan Printing Co., Ltd., Japan

CONTENTS

TO THE READER

Ireland is a small country in transition from a glorious but troubled past to a bright future. Thirty years ago, during my first visit, the past seemed dominant: Dublin was a Georgian city, shabby, dignified; the countryside was covered with castles and ruins—some of them inhabited by people, others by livestock; and the literary talk was full of anecdotes about Joyce and Yeats (and earlier writers) as though they were still with us. During my most recent visit, I have sensed a new vitality, not only in Dublin and Belfast, but also in smaller cities and towns. Some of the old castles are restored and open to the public, but many of the ruins evidently have been removed, so that the countryside no longer looks like an outdoor museum. The anecdotes deal with younger writers (not necessarily Irish), with fresh ideas, with broader horizons, such as the opening up of the European economy in 1992. One Irishman told me, "I was glad to have a bicycle. My son owns a car. My grandson is learning to fly a plane."

But there is more to this transition than changes in conversation, buildings, or transportation. Irish society is being transformed, with new roles for women, government, the elderly, the Church. Britain (formerly England) is no longer looked upon as the ruler of Ireland's destiny. Invasions, if they are peaceful, and well capitalized, are welcome. Exports are increasing. And the fearful draining away of young people—to London, to America, to any place that could promise a job and a future—is lessening. Some of the far-flung millions of Irish-Americans, Irish-Canadians, Irish-Australians, and people of Irish ancestry in other countries are beginning to think about going home—for a visit, for a semester, for retirement perhaps. Brian Coffey, born in Ireland and living in Missouri, wrote that he loved his new home,

> yet I am charmed
> by the hills behind Dublin,
> those white stone cottages,
> grass green as no other green is green,
> my mother's people, their ways.

This kind of nostalgia is felt by people all over the world, all the more keenly because Ireland's past has been so troubled. "Wherever green is worn," said Yeats, "a terrible beauty is born," not the green of grass, but the patriotic green of Irish uniforms and flags, not simply the beauty of Irish countryside or cities or people, but the painful beauty arising from warfare, persecution, famine, and worse.

Recently, however, I ventured into Northern Ireland for the first time and found the country and the people there also to my liking. They welcomed me as an American (not as an Irishman, despite my name) and I regarded them as Irish (despite the differences in religion, politics, and other things). I don't know how or when it will happen, but sooner or later a unification must be achieved. A terrible beauty is born wherever orange, the traditional color of the North, is worn, and everyone I met, on either side of any line, has clearly had enough terror. In this book, therefore, I bring together poetry and art from Northern Ireland as well as from "the South," the Republic. The perspectives are very different, in some instances, but they are perspectives about a common past, present, and future. Natalie Hardwick, a Belfast schoolgirl, writes:

Bomb City, Bomb City, Bomb City drummed into us, Night and Day minute by minute.
Strangers pity and question: How can we poor, terrorised people live surrounded by bigotry, bombs and bullets?

I don't know the answer, but I hope that her generation will find it. Letting go of the past, living in the present, building a future with benefits for all—this may be the way to peace.

"Ireland *in* poetry?" a friend said, looking at my manuscript. "But Ireland *is* poetry." So it seems at times, with the country and its literature as closely interwoven as the decorations on the *Tara Brooch* or *The Book of Kells.* I don't agree with Auden, who said, in his tribute to Yeats, that "poetry makes nothing happen." Much Irish poetry has been written provocatively, to stir up feelings, to keep them alive, to make all sorts of things happen, or happen again.

Yet some Irish poetry is more like a record of events and personal reactions, or a reflection on what is past, or passing, or to come. No moment is too brief, no object or happening too insignificant, for a poet to notice it. Patrick Kavanagh wrote, in "Spraying the Potatoes":

> The flocks of green potato-stalks
> Were blossom spread for sudden flight,
> The Kerr's Pinks in a frivelled blue,
> The Arran Banners wearing white.

This may be considered typical of the "new" Irish poetry that is simpler, more lyrical, more immediate than earlier work, yet it reminds me of really old poems, such as "The Hermitage," translated by Frank O'Connor, in which the writer seeks:

> A pleasant woodland all about
>   To shield it from the wind,
> And make a home for singing birds
>   Before it and behind.
>
> A southern aspect for the heat,
>   A stream along its foot,
> A smooth green lawn with rich top soil
>   Propitious to all fruit.

Just the sort of place that you or I might like to find, as we take part in Ireland's sunny future.

This book is divided into four main parts. First, the country of Ireland includes sections on natural beauty, castles, churches and cathedrals, cities and towns, and rural life. Second, the history of Ireland includes sections on Ireland as a goddess, the Celtic heritage, religion, wars and invasions, and the orange and green. Third, the people of Ireland includes sections on Yeats ("A Poet's Life"), Dubliners and other individuals, relationships, the generations, Irish wit and wisdom, nostalgia and "The American Connection." Finally, part four deals with the future of Ireland, with sections on children and prosperity and peace.

More than 150 poems have been selected for this book, including work by John Montague, Louis MacNeice, Derek Mahon, Samuel Beckett, Jonathan Swift, James Joyce, Eavan Boland, Seamus Heaney, Rudyard Kipling, Ted Hughes, Thomas Moore, James Clarence Mangan, Katherine Tynan, and John Synge. Accompanying their poems are numerous examples of Irish art from museums, galleries, and private collections throughout Ireland and America. Individual artists include Louis LeBrocquy, Paul Henry, Walter Osborne, Sir Frederick Burton, William Orpen, Jack B. Yeats and John Butler Yeats, Roderic O'Conor, Harry Clarke, Sir John Lavery, Joan Walsh-Smith, and Jane Morgan.

A great many people, including museum and library officials, poets and artists, editors and bookstore owners, pedestrians and potentates, helped in one way or another to make this book possible. I am especially grateful to Paul Gottlieb, my friend and publisher, who has the vision to see what success may be in store for books of poetry and art. Lois Brown was again a great source of wise guidance and good humor during the editorial process. Among other fine people at Abrams, my thanks to Carol Robson for designing another beautiful book; to John Crowley, for giving me the benefit of his experience in tracking down the many paintings, photographs, and other works of art; and to Margaret Rennolds, for seeing the book through to completion. Fifi Oscard, my literary agent, has also been very helpful. Thanks to all!

CHARLES SULLIVAN
WASHINGTON, D.C.

THE LAKE ISLE OF INNISFREE

W . B . YEATS (1865 – 1939)

I will arise and go now, and go to Innisfree,
And a small cabin build there, of clay and wattles made:
Nine bean-rows will I have there, a hive for the honeybee,
And live alone in the bee-loud glade.

And I shall have some peace there, for peace comes dropping slow,
Dropping from the veils of the morning to where the cricket sings;
There midnight's all a glimmer, and noon a purple glow,
And evening full of the linnet's wings.

I will arise and go now, for always night and day
I hear lake water lapping with low sounds by the shore;
While I stand on the roadway, or on the pavements grey,
I hear it in the deep heart's core.

LOUGH GILL, COUNTY SLIGO by Jack B. Yeats. 1906.
Watercolor on paper. The National Gallery of Ireland, Dublin

The artist, brother of the poet Yeats, has depicted the lake in which "Innisfree" is situated.

THE GLENS

JOHN HEWITT (BORN 1907)

Groined by deep glens and walled along the west
by the bare hilltops and the tufted moors,
this rim of arable that ends in foam
has but to drop a leaf or snap a branch
and my hand twitches with the leaping verse
as hazel twig will wrench the straining wrists
for untapped jet that thrusts beneath the sod.

Not these my people, of a vainer faith
and a more violent lineage. My dead
lie in the steepled hillock of Kilmore
in a fat country rich with bloom and fruit.
My days, the busy days I owe the world,
are bound to paved unerring roads and rooms
heavy with talk of politics and art.
I cannot spare more than a common phrase
of crops and weather when I pace these lanes
and pause at hedge gap spying on their skill,
so many fences stretch between our minds.

I fear their creed as we have always feared
the lifted hand between the mind and truth.
I know their savage history of wrong
and would at moments lend an eager voice,
if voice avail, to set that tally straight.

And yet no other corner in this land
offers in shape and colour all I need
for sight to torch the mind with living light.

A DAY IN AUGUST

FRANK ORMSBY (BORN 1947)

And still no stronger. Swathed in rugs he lingered
    Near to the windows, gauging distant hills.
Balked by the panes that promised light and flowers,
    The wasps were dying furiously on sills.

A doctor called. She walked him to the doorstep,
    Then sent the children out to gather cones
Under the trees beside the ruined churchyard.
    They romped, unheeding, in the tilted stones.

And now the wheels are turning. They impress
    Tracks that will not outlast the winter's rain.
The siren leaves a wash of emptiness.
    He is lost to the small farms, lane by lane.

THE STRAND

MICHAEL LONGLEY (BORN 1939)

I discover, remaindered from yesterday,
Cattle tracks, a sanderling's tiny trail,
The footprints of the children and my own
Linking the dunes to the water's edge,
Reducing to sand the dry shells, the toe-
And fingernail parings of the sea.

An Irish beach. Photograph by Jill Uris

Ruins of an Elizabethan manor house on the site of Dunboy Castle, Co. Cork.
Photograph by Jill Uris

WINDHARP

JOHN MONTAGUE (BORN 1929)

FOR PATRICK COLLINS

The sounds of Ireland,
that restless whispering
you never get away
from, seeping out of
low bushes and grass,
heatherbells and fern,
wrinkling bog pools,
scraping tree branches,
light hunting cloud,
sound hounding sight,
a hand ceaselessly
combing and stroking
the landscape, till
the valley gleams
like the pile upon
a mountain pony's coat.

PRELUDE

JOHN M. SYNGE (1871–1909)

Still south I went and west and south again,
Through Wicklow from the morning till the night,
And far from cities, and the sites of men,
Lived with the sunshine and the moon's delight.

I knew the stars, the flowers, and the birds,
The grey and wintry sides of many glens,
And did but half remember human words,
In converse with the mountains, moors, and fens.

SKETCH PORTRAITS OF J. M. SYNGE
by Jack B. Yeats. c. 1905.
Pencil on paper. Collection Anne Yeats, Dublin

J. M. Synge

THE TROUT
JOHN MONTAGUE (BORN 1929)

Flat on the bank I parted
Rushes to ease my hands
In the water without a ripple
And tilt them slowly downstream
To where he lay, tendril light,
In his fluid sensual dream.

Bodiless lord of creation
I hung briefly above him
Savouring my own absence
Senses expanding in the slow
Motion, the photographic calm
That grows before action.

As the curve of my hands
Swung under his body
He surged, with visible pleasure.
I was so preternaturally close
I could count every stipple
But still cast no shadow, until

The two palms crossed in a cage
Under the lightly pulsing gills.
Then (entering my own enlarged
Shape, which rode on the water)
I gripped. To this day I can
Taste his terror on my hands.

THE PENINSULA
SEAMUS HEANEY (BORN 1939)

When you have nothing more to say, just drive
For a day all round the peninsula.
The sky is tall as over a runway,
The land without marks so you will not arrive

But pass through, though always skirting landfall.
At dusk, horizons drink down sea and hill,
The ploughed field swallows the whitewashed gable
And you're in the dark again. Now recall

The glazed foreshore and silhouetted log,
That rock where breakers shredded into rags,
The leggy birds stilted on their own legs,
Islands riding themselves out into the fog

And drive back home, still with nothing to say
Except that now you will uncode all landscapes
By this: things founded clean on their own shapes,
Water and ground in their extremity.

Slea Head, Dingle Peninsula, Co. Kerry.
Photograph by Kathleen Jo Ryan

THE MEETING OF THE WATERS
THOMAS MOORE (1779–1852)

There is not in the wide world a valley so sweet
As that vale in whose bosom the bright waters meet;
Oh! the last rays of feeling and life must depart,
Ere the bloom of that valley shall fade from my heart.

Yet it *was* not that Nature had shed o'er the scene
Her purest of crystal and brightest of green;
'Twas *not* her soft magic of streamlet or hill,
Oh! no,—it was something more exquisite still.

'Twas that friends, the belov'd of my bosom, were near,
Who made every dear scene of enchantment more dear,
And who felt how the best charms of nature improve,
When we see them reflected from looks that we love.

Sweet vale of Avoca! how calm could I rest
In thy bosom of shade, with the friends I love best,
Where the storms that we feel in this cold world should cease,
And our hearts, like thy waters, be mingled in peace.

THE BLACKBIRD
BY BELFAST LOUGH
TRANSLATED FROM THE EARLY IRISH
BY FRANK O'CONNOR (1903–1966)

What little throat
Has framed that note?
What gold beak shot
   It far away?
A blackbird on
His leafy throne
Tossed it alone
   Across the bay.

A WARNING TO CONQUERORS

DONAGH MACDONAGH (1912–1968)

This is the country of the Norman tower,
The graceless keep, the bleak and slitted eye
Where fear drove comfort out; straw on the floor
Was price of conquering security.

They came and won, and then for centuries
Stood to their arms; the face grew bleak and lengthened
In the night vigil, while their foes at ease
Sang of the stranger and the towers he strengthened.

Ragweed and thistle hold the Norman field
And cows the hall where Gaelic never rang
Melodiously to harp or spinning wheel.
Their songs are spent now with the voice that sang;

And lost their conquest. This soft land quietly
Engulfed them like the Saxon and the Dane—
But kept the jutted brow, the slitted eye;
Only the faces and the names remain.

Clonony Castle, Co. Offaly. Photograph by George Mott

THE DANCE HALF DONE
MARY ANN LARKIN (BORN 1945)

Our fate was settled centuries ago
when the huge floes cracked
loosening mist upon the island
sealing in
the flow of light over distances
herons in green-grey waters
a girl's red hair
falling from the turret
The island itself suspended
in a primal sac of light
fed by a dark cord from within the bog

Poets send their words into the mist
in this land where symbols live—
like a dance behind a grey scrim
a promise unfulfilled
a yes or a no never said
just as the mouth begins to form the words
as the heron lifts its leg
the girl her comb

We are stamped by this
land of murmurs and half-heard chants
a dreaminess in our gaze
hands caught in mid-air
eyes following a passage of light
The young women wrap themselves in grey wool
and go walking
The young men watch

We remember
the dance half-done
the kiss almost given
the red hair falling from the turret
hear, above grey waters,
the half-promise of the lute

HELELLIL AND HILDEBRAND or
THE MEETING ON THE TURRET STAIRS
by Sir Frederick Burton. 1864.
Watercolor on paper.
The National Gallery of Ireland, Dublin

TO BE CARVED ON A STONE
AT THOOR BALLYLEE
W. B. YEATS (1865–1939)

I, the poet William Yeats,
With old mill boards and sea-green slates,
And smithy work from the Gort forge,
Restored this tower for my wife George;
And may these characters remain
When all is ruin once again.

19

DOWAGER

JOHN MONTAGUE (BORN 1929)

I dwell in this leaky Western castle.
American matrons weave across the carpet,
Sorefooted as camels, and less useful.

Smooth Ionic columns hold up a roof.
A chandelier shines on a foxhound's coat:
The grandson of a grandmother I reared.

In the old days I read or embroidered,
But now it is enough to see the sky change,
Clouds extend or smother a mountain's shape.

Wet afternoons I ride in the Rolls;
Windshield wipers flail helpless against the rain:
I thrash through pools like smashing panes of glass.

And the light afterwards! Hedges steam,
I ride through a damp tunnel of sweetness,
The bonnet strewn with bridal hawthorn

From which a silver lady leaps, always young.
Alone, I hum with satisfaction in the sun,
An old bitch, with a warm mouthful of game.

Kissing the Blarney Stone. Photograph. c. 1870

BLARNEY CASTLE

FATHER PROUT (1804–1866)

(FRANCIS SYLVESTER MAHONY)

There is a boat on the lake to float on,
And lots of beauties which I can't entwine;
But were I a preacher, or a classic teacher,
In every feature I'd make 'em shine!

There is a stone there, that whoever kisses,
O! he never misses to grow eloquent;
'Tis he may clamber to a lady's chamber,
Or become a member of parliament:

A clever spouter he'll soon turn out, or
An out-and-outer, "to be let alone."
Don't hope to hinder him, or to bewilder him,
Sure he's a pilgrim from the Blarney stone!

CLONMACNOISE
TRANSLATED FROM THE EARLY IRISH BY T. W. ROLLESTON (1857–1920)

In a quiet water'd land, a land of roses,
　Stands Saint Kieran's city fair;
And the warriors of Erin in their famous generations
　Slumber there.

There beneath the dewy hillside sleep the noblest
　Of the clan of Conn,
Each below his stone with name in branching Ogham
　And the sacred knot thereon.

There they laid to rest the seven Kings of Tara,
　There the sons of Cairbrè sleep—
Battle-banners of the Gael that in Kieran's plain of crosses
　Now their final hosting keep.

And in Clonmacnoise they laid the men of Teffia,
　And right many a lord of Breagh;
Deep the sod above Clan Creidè and Clan Conaill,
　Kind in hall and fierce in fray.

Many and many a son of Conn the Hundred-fighter
　In the red earth lies at rest;
Many a blue eye of Clan Colman the turf covers,
　Many a swan-white breast.

Ruins of Clonmacnoise, Co. Offaly.
Photograph by Kathleen Jo Ryan

The Rock of Cashel, Co. Tipperary.
Photograph by Kathleen Jo Ryan

THE ROCK OF CASHEL

SIR AUBREY DE VERE (1788–1846)

Royal and saintly Cashel! I would gaze
   Upon the wreck of thy departed powers,
   Not in the dewy light of matin hours,
Nor the meridian pomp of summer's blaze,
But at the close of dim autumnal days,
   When the sun's parting glance, through slanting showers,
   Sheds o'er thy rock-throned battlements and towers
Such awful gleams as brighten o'er Decay's
Prophetic cheek. At such a time, methinks,
   There breathes from thy lone courts and voiceless aisles
A melancholy moral, such as sinks
   On the lone traveller's heart, amid the piles
Of vast Persepolis on her mountain stand,
Or Thebes half buried in the desert sand.

IN THE CATHEDRAL CLOSE

EDWARD DOWDEN (1843 – 1913)

In the Dean's porch a nest of clay
 With five small tenants may be seen,
Five solemn faces, each as wise
 As though its owner were a Dean;

Five downy fledglings in a row,
 Packed close, as in the antique pew
The schoolgirls are whose foreheads clear
 At the *Venite* shine on you.

Day after day the swallows sit
 With scarce a stir, with scarce a sound,
But dreaming and digesting much
 They grow thus wise and soft and round.

They watch the Canons come to dine,
 And hear, the mullion-bars across,
Over the fragrant fruit and wine
 Deep talk of rood-screen and reredos.

Her hands with field-flowers drenched, a child
 Leaps past in wind-blown dress and hair,
The swallows turn their heads askew—
 Five judges deem that she is fair.

Prelusive touches sound within,
 Straightway they recognize the sign,
And, blandly nodding, they approve
 The minuet of Rubinstein.

They mark the cousins' schoolboy talk,
 (Male birds flown wide from minster bell)
And blink at each broad term of art,
 Binomial or bicycle.

Ah! downy young ones, soft and warm,
 Doth such a stillness mask from sight
Such swiftness? can such peace conceal
 Passion and ecstasy of flight?

Yet somewhere 'mid your Eastern suns,
 Under a white Greek architrave
At morn, or when the shaft of fire
 Lies large upon the Indian wave,

A sense of something dear gone-by
 Will stir, strange longings thrill the heart
For a small world embowered and close,
 Of which ye some time were a part.

The dew-drench'd flowers, the child's glad eyes,
 Your joy unhuman shall control,
And in your wings a light and wind
 Shall move from the Maestro's soul.

ST. PATRICK'S CLOSE, DUBLIN by Walter Osborne.
1887. Oil on canvas.
The National Gallery of Ireland, Dublin

DUBLIN

LOUIS MACNEICE (1907–1963)

Grey brick upon brick,
Declamatory bronze
On sombre pedestals—
O'Connell, Grattan, Moore—
And the brewery tugs and the swans
On the balustraded stream
And the bare bones of a fanlight
Over a hungry door
And the air soft on the cheek
And porter running from the taps
With a head of yellow cream
And Nelson on his pillar
Watching his world collapse.

This was never my town,
I was not born nor bred
Nor schooled here and she will not
Have me alive or dead
But yet she holds my mind
With her seedy elegance,
With her gentle veils of rain
And all her ghosts that walk
And all that hide behind
Her Georgian façades—
The catcalls and the pain,
The glamour of her squalor,
The bravado of her talk.

The lights jig in the river
With a concertina movement
And the sun comes up in the morning
Like barley-sugar on the water
And the mist on the Wicklow hills
Is close, as close
As the peasantry were to the landlord,
As the Irish to the Anglo-Irish,
As the killer is close one moment
To the man he kills,
Or as the moment itself
Is close to the next moment.

She is not an Irish town
And she is not English,
Historic with guns and vermin
And the cold renown
Of a fragment of Church latin,
Of an oratorical phrase.
But oh the days are soft,
Soft enough to forget
The lesson better learnt,
The bullet on the wet
Streets, the crooked deal,
The steel behind the laugh,
The Four Courts burnt.

Fort of the Dane,
Garrison of the Saxon,
Augustan capital
Of a Gaelic nation,
Appropriating all
The alien brought,
You give me time for thought
And by a juggler's trick
You poise the toppling hour—
O greyness run to flower,
Grey stone, grey water,
And brick upon grey brick.

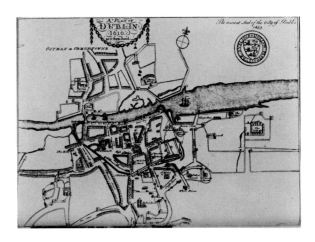

Map of Dublin.
Engraving by John Speed. 1610.
National Library of Ireland, Dublin

The Four Courts of Dublin.
Photograph by Owen D. Edwards

IF EVER YOU GO TO DUBLIN TOWN

PATRICK KAVANAGH (1904–1967)

If ever you go to Dublin town
In a hundred years or so
Inquire for me in Baggot Street
And what I was like to know.
O he was a queer one,
Fol dol the di do,
He was a queer one
I tell you.

My great-grandmother knew him well,
He asked her to come and call
On him in his flat and she giggled at the thought
Of a young girl's lovely fall.
O he was dangerous,
Fol dol the di do,
He was dangerous
I tell you.

On Pembroke Road look out for my ghost,
Dishevelled with shoes untied,
Playing through the railings with little children
Whose children have long since died.
O he was a nice man,
Fol dol the di do,
He was a nice man
I tell you.

Go into a pub and listen well
If my voice still echoes there,
Ask the men what their grandsires thought
And tell them to answer fair.
O he was eccentric,
Fol dol the di do,
He was eccentric
I tell you.

He had the knack of making men feel
As small as they really were
Which meant as great as God had made them
But as males they disliked his air.
O he was a proud one,
Fol dol the di do,
He was a proud one
I tell you.

If ever you go to Dublin town
In a hundred years or so
Sniff for my personality,
Is it Vanity's vapour now?
O he was a vain one,
Fol dol the di do,
He was a vain one
I tell you.

I saw his name with a hundred others
In a book in the library,
It said he had never fully achieved
His potentiality.
O he was slothful,
Fol dol the di do,
He was slothful
I tell you.

He knew that posterity has no use
For anything but the soul,
The lines that speak the passionate heart,
The spirit that lives alone.
O he was a lone one,
Fol dol the di do
Yet he lived happily
I tell you.

THE LIFFEY SWIM by Jack B. Yeats.
1923. Oil on canvas.
The National Gallery of Ireland, Dublin

REVERIE by Marjorie Robinson.
1914. Watercolor on ivory.
Ulster Museum, Belfast

THE KING'S HORSES
JOHN HEWITT (BORN 1907)

After fifty years, nearly, I remember,
living then in a quiet leafy suburb,
waking in the darkness, made aware
of a continuous irregular noise,
and groping to the side-window to discover
the shadow-shapes which made that muffled patter
passing across the end of our avenue,
the black trees and the streetlights shuttering
a straggle of flowing shadows, endless, of horses.

Gypsies they could have been, or tinkers maybe,
mustering to some hosting of their clans,
or horse-dealers heading their charges to the docks
timed to miss the day's traffic and alarms;
a migration the newspapers had not foretold;
some battle's ragged finish, dream repeated;
the last of an age retreating, withdrawing,
leaving us beggared, bereft
of the proud nodding muzzles, the nervous bodies;
gone from us the dark men with their ancient skills
of saddle and stirrup, of bridle and breeding.

It was an end, I was sure, but an end of what
I never could tell. It was never reported;
but the echoing hooves persisted. Years after,
in a London hotel in the grey dawn
a serious man concerned with certain duties,
I heard again the metal clatter of hooves staccato
and hurriedly rose to catch a glimpse of my horses,
but the pace and beat were utterly different:
I saw by the men astride these were the King's horses
going about the King's business, never mine.

SETTLERS
TOM PAULIN (BORN 1949)

They cross from Glasgow to a black city
   Of gantries, mills and steeples. They begin to belong.
He manages the Iceworks, is an elder of the Kirk;
   She becomes, briefly, a cook in Carson's Army.
Some mornings, walking through the company gate,
   He touches the bonnet of a brown lorry.
It is warm. The men watch and say nothing.
   "Queer, how it runs off in the night,"
He says to McCullough, then climbs to his office.
   He stores a warm knowledge on his palm.

Nightlandings on the Antrim coast, the movement of guns
   Now snug in their oiled paper below the floors
Of sundry kirks and tabernacles in that county.

CAVE

FROM THE CAVE OF NIGHT

JOHN MONTAGUE (BORN 1929)

FOR SEAN LUCY

*Men who believe in absurdities
will commit atrocities.*

VOLTAIRE

The rifled honeycomb
of the high-rise hotel
where a wind tunnel moans.
While jungleclad troops
ransack the Falls, race
through huddled streets,
we lie awake, the wide
window washed with rain,
your oval face, and tide
of yellow hair luminous
as you turn to me again
seeking refuge as the
cave of night blooms
with fresh explosions.

FROM AFTERLIVES

DEREK MAHON (BORN 1941)

I am going home by sea
For the first time in years.
Somebody thumbs a guitar
On the dark deck, while a gull
Dreams at the masthead,
The moon-splashed waves exult.

At dawn the ship trembles, turns
In a wide arc to back
Shuddering up the grey lough
Past lightship and buoy,
Slipway and dry dock
Where a naked bulb burns;

And I step ashore in a fine rain
To a city so changed
By five years of war
I scarcely recognise
The places I grew up in,
The faces that try to explain.

But the hills are still the same
Grey-blue above Belfast.
Perhaps if I'd stayed behind
And lived it bomb by bomb
I might have grown up at last
And learnt what is meant by home.

THE WOMEN OF BELFAST (NO. 7)
by F. E. McWilliam. 1972. Bronze.
Ulster Museum, Belfast

THE OTHER SIDE

NATALIE HARDWICK (BORN C. 1975)

Bomb City, Bomb City, Bomb City drummed into us, Night and Day
    minute by minute.
Strangers pity and question: How can we poor, terrorised people live
    surrounded by bigotry, bombs and bullets?

How blind and brainwashed people are. How the media manipulate
    and condition people's minds.

Oh yes, They report the raids and the retaliations—one for one—tit for
    tat. They show the broken homes and the broken hearts, but that's it;
    nothing else. Why, so many ask, not include the life with the death,
    the beauty with the bombs, the joy with the despair and the love
    with the hate. Yet this story is never told.

THE BOMB DISPOSAL

CIARAN CARSON (BORN 1948)

Is it just like picking a lock
with the slow deliberation of a funeral,
hesitating through a darkened nave
until you find the answer?

Listening to the malevolent tick
of its heart, can you read
the message of the threaded veins
like print, its body's chart?

The city is a map of the city,
its forbidden areas changing daily.
I find myself in a crowded taxi
making deviations from the known route,

ending in a cul-de-sac
where everyone breaks out suddenly
in whispers, noting the boarded windows,
the drawn blinds.

Young man attacking British military vehicle, Ballymurphy, Northern Ireland. 1981.
Photograph © James Nachtwey Magnum Photos

DERRY
SEAMUS DEANE (BORN 1940)

I

The unemployment in our bones
Erupting on our hands in stones;

The thought of violence a relief,
The act of violence a grief;

Our bitterness and love
Hand in glove.

II

At the very most
The mind's eye
Perceives the ghost
Of the hands try
To timidly knock
On the walled rock.
But nothing will come
And the hands become
As they insist
Mailed fists.

III

The Scots and English
Settling for the best.
The unfriendly natives
Ready for the worst.
It has been like this for years
Someone says,
It might be so forever, someone fears,
Or for days.

DERRY MORNING

DEREK MAHON (BORN 1941)

The mist clears and the cavities
Glow black in the rubbled city's
Broken mouth. An early crone,
Muse of a fitful revolution
Wasted by the fray, she sees
Her *aisling* falter in the breeze,
Her oak-grove vision hesitate
By empty wharf and city gate.

Here it began, and here at least
It fades into the finite past
Or seems to: clattering shadows whop
Mechanically over pub and shop.
A strangely pastoral silence rules
The shining roofs and murmuring schools;
For this is how the centuries work—
Two steps forward, one step back.

Hard to believe this tranquil place,
Its desolation almost peace,
Was recently a boom-town wild
With expectation, each unscheduled
Incident a measurable
Tremor on the Richter Scale
Of world events, each vibrant scene
Translated to the drizzling screen.

What of the change envisioned here,
The quantum leap from fear to fire?
Smoke from a thousand chimneys strains
One way beneath the returning rains
That shroud the bomb-sites, while the fog
Of time receives the ideologue.
A Russian freighter bound for home
Mourns to the city in its gloom.

37

RETURN

SEAMUS DEANE (BORN 1940)

The train shot through the dark.
Hedges leapt across the window-pane.
Trees belled in foliage were stranded,
Inarticulate with rain.
A blur of lighted farm implied
The evacuated countryside.

I am appalled by its emptiness.
Every valley glows with pain
As we run like a current through;
Then the memories darken again.
In this Irish past I dwell
Like sound implicit in a bell.

The train curves round a river,
And how tenderly its gouts of steam
Contemplate the nodding moon
The waters from the clouds redeem.
Two hours from Belfast
I am snared in my past.

Crusts of light lie pulsing
Diamanté with the rain
At the track's end. Amazing!
I am in Derry once again.
Once more I turn to greet
Ground that flees from my feet.

HARRIET ANNE, COUNTESS OF BELFAST by Thomas Lawrence.
Before 1825. Oil on canvas. Ulster Museum, Belfast

OLD BAAL'S BRIDGE, LIMERICK by James Henry Brocas.
Early 19th century. Ink and watercolor on paper.
The National Gallery of Ireland, Dublin

THE LIMERICK HELL FIRE CLUB
by James Worsdale. Early 18th century. Oil on canvas.
The National Gallery of Ireland, Dublin

FROM **A POEM**
DEDICATED TO MRS. BLENNERHASSET,
THE ONLY FEMALE MEMBER
OF THE LIMERICK HELL FIRE CLUB
DANIEL HAYES (18TH CENTURY)

But if in endless Drinking you delight
Croker will ply you till you sink outright
Croker for swilling Floods of Wine renowned
Whose matchless Board with various plenty crowned
Eternal Scenes of Riot, Mirth and Noise
With all the thunder of the Nenagh Boys
We laugh we roar, the ceaseless Bumpers fly
Till the sun purples o'er the Morning sky
And if unruly Passions chance to rise
A willing Wench the Firgrove still supplies.

41

THE SWEETNESS OF NATURE

TRANSLATED FROM THE IRISH (C. 12TH CENTURY)

BY FRANK O'CONNOR (1903–1966)

Endlessly over the water
    Birds of the Bann are singing;
Sweeter to me their voices
    Than any churchbell's ringing.

Over the plain of Moyra
    Under the heels of foemen
I saw my people broken
    As flax is scutched by women.

But the cries I hear by Derry
    Are not of men triumphant;
I hear their calls in the evening,
    Swans calm and exultant.

I hear the stag's belling
    Over the valley's steepness;
No music on the earth
    Can move me like its sweetness.

Christ, Christ hear me!
    Christ, Christ of Thy meekness!
Christ, Christ love me!
    Sever me not from Thy sweetness!

THE BELLS OF SHANDON

FATHER PROUT (1804–1866)

(FRANCIS SYLVESTER MAHONY)

With deep affection and recollection
    I often think of the Shandon bells,
Whose sounds so wild would, in days of childhood,
    Fling round my cradle their magic spells.
On this I ponder, where'er I wander,
    And thus grow fonder, sweet Cork, of thee;
        With thy bells of Shandon,
        That sound so grand on
The pleasant waters of the river Lee.

I have heard bells chiming full many a clime in,
    Tolling sublime in cathedral shrine;
While at a glib rate brass tongues would vibrate,
    But all their music spoke nought to thine;
For memory dwelling on each proud swelling
    Of thy belfry knelling its bold notes free,
        Made the bells of Shandon
        Sound far more grand on
The pleasant waters of the river Lee.

I have heard bells tolling "old Adrian's mole" in,
    Their thunder rolling from the Vatican,
With cymbals glorious, swinging uproarious
    In the gorgeous turrets of Notre Dame;
But thy sounds were sweeter than the dome of Peter
    Flings o'er the Tiber, pealing solemnly.
        Oh! the bells of Shandon
        Sound far more grand on
The pleasant waters of the river Lee.

There's a bell in Moscow, while on tower and Kiosko
    In St. Sophia the Turkman gets,
And loud in air calls men to prayer
    From the tapering summit of tall minarets.
Such empty phantom I freely grant 'em,
    But there's an anthem more dear to me:
        'Tis the bells of Shandon,
        That sound so grand on
The pleasant waters of the river Lee.

THE VILLAGE

OLIVER GOLDSMITH (1728 – 1774)

Sweet was the sound, when oft at evening's close
Up yonder hill the village murmur rose;
There, as I passed with careless steps and slow,
The mingling notes came soften'd from below:
The swain responsive as the milkmaid sung,
The sober herd that low'd to meet their young;
The noisy geese that gabbled o'er the pool,
The playful children just let loose from school;
The watchdog's voice that bay'd the whisp'ring wind,
And the loud laugh that spoke the vacant mind;
These all in sweet confusion sought the shade,
And fill'd each pause the nightingale had made.
But now the sounds of population fail,
No cheerful murmurs fluctuate in the gale,
No busy steps the grass-grown footway tread,
For all the bloomy flush of life is fled.
All but yon widow'd, solitary thing,
That feebly bends beside the plashy spring:
She, wretched matron, forc'd in age, for bread,
To strip the brook with mantling cresses spread,
To strip her wintry faggot from the thorn,
To seek her nightly shed, and weep till morn;
She only left of all the harmless train,
The sad historian of the pensive plain.

Near Brandon, Co. Kerry.
Photograph by Robin Morrison

FOLLOWER

SEAMUS HEANEY (BORN 1939)

My father worked with a horse-plough,
His shoulders globed like a full sail strung
Between the shafts and the furrow.
The horses strained at his clicking tongue.

An expert. He would set the wing
And fit the bright steel-pointed sock.
The sod rolled over without breaking.
At the headrig, with a single pluck

Of reins, the sweating team turned round
And back into the land. His eye
Narrowed and angled at the ground,
Mapping the furrow exactly.

I stumbled in his hob-nailed wake,
Fell sometimes on the polished sod;
Sometimes he rode me on his back
Dipping and rising to his plod.

I wanted to grow up and plough,
To close one eye, stiffen my arm.
All I ever did was follow
In his broad shadow round the farm.

I was a nuisance, tripping, falling,
Yapping always. But today
It is my father who keeps stumbling
Behind me, and will not go away.

PORTRAIT OF SEAMUS HEANEY
by Edward McGuire. 1974.
Oil on canvas.
Ulster Museum, Belfast

DIGGING

SEAMUS HEANEY (BORN 1939)

Between my finger and my thumb
The squat pen rests; snug as a gun.

Under my window, a clean rasping sound
When the spade sinks into gravelly ground:
My father, digging. I look down

Till his straining rump among the flowerbeds
Bends low, comes up twenty years away
Stooping in rhythm through potato drills
Where he was digging.

The coarse boot nestled on the lug, the shaft
Against the inside knee was levered firmly.
He rooted out tall tops, buried the bright edge deep
To scatter new potatoes that we picked
Loving their cool hardness in our hands.

By God, the old man could handle a spade.
Just like his old man.

My grandfather cut more turf in a day
Than any other man on Toner's bog.
Once I carried him milk in a bottle
Corked sloppily with paper. He straightened up
To drink it, then fell to right away

Nicking and slicing neatly, heaving sods
Over his shoulder, going down and down
For the good turf. Digging.

The cold smell of potato mould, the squelch and slap
Of soggy peat, the curt cuts of an edge
Through living roots awaken in my head.
But I've no spade to follow men like them.

Between my finger and my thumb
The squat pen rests.
I'll dig with it.

OLD ROADS

EILEAN NÍ CHUILLEANÁIN (BORN 1942)

Missing from the map, the abandoned roads
Reach across the mountain, threading into
Clefts and valleys, shuffle between thick
Hedges of flowery thorn.
The grass flows into tracks of wheels,
Mowed evenly by the careful sheep;
Drenched, it guards the gaps of silence
Only trampled on the pattern day.

And if, an odd time, late
At night, a cart passes
Splashing in a burst stream, crunching bones,
The wavering candle hung by the shaft
Slaps light against a single gable
Catches a flat tombstone
Shaking a nervous beam in a white face

Their arthritic fingers
Their stiffening grasp cannot
Hold long on the hillside —
Slowly the old roads lose their grip.

Ruin, Co. Kerry.
Photograph by Richard Fitzgerald

LAKESIDE COTTAGES by Paul Henry.
Early 20th century. Oil on canvas.
The Hugh Lane Municipal Gallery
of Modern Art, Dublin

SHANCODUFF

PATRICK KAVANAGH (1904–1967)

My black hills have never seen the sun rising,
Eternally they look north towards Armagh.
Lot's wife would not be salt if she had been
Incurious as my black hills that are happy
When dawn whitens Glassdrummond chapel.

My hills hoard the bright shillings of March
While the sun searches in every pocket.
They are my Alps and I have climbed the Matterhorn
With a sheaf of hay for three perishing calves
In the field under the Big Forth of Rocksavage.

The sleety winds fondle the rushy beards of Shancoduff
While the cattle-drovers sheltering in the Featherna Bush
Look up and say: "Who owns them hungry hills
That the water-hen and snipe must have forsaken?
A poet? Then by heavens he must be poor."
I hear and is my heart not badly shaken?

FIELD DAY

W. R. RODGERS (1909–1969)

The old farmer, nearing death, asked
To be carried outside and set down
Where he could see a certain field
"And then I will cry my heart out," he said.

It troubles me, thinking about that man;
What shape was the field of his crying
In Donegal?

I remember a small field in Down, a field
Within fields, shaped like a triangle.
I could have stood there and looked at it
All day long.

And I remember crossing the frontier between
France and Spain at a forbidden point, and seeing
A small triangular field in Spain,
And stopping

Or walking in Ireland down any rutted by-road
To where it hit the highway, there was always
At this turning-point and abutment
A still centre, a V-shape of grass
Untouched by cornering traffic,
Where country lads larked at night.

I think I know what the shape of the field was
That made the old man weep.

THE WAKE by Nathaniel Grogan. Oil on canvas. c. 1795.
Private collection, Ireland

On the roadside: tinker fixing pot with family in background; Co. Waterford.
Photograph by Richard Fitzgerald

THE BALLAD OF THE TINKER'S WIFE

SIGERSON CLIFFORD (1913–1985)

When cocks curved throats for crowing
And cows in slumber kneeled,
She tiptoed out the half-door
And crossed her father's field.

Down the mountain shoulders
The ragged dawnlight came
And a cold wind from the westland
Blew out the last star's flame.

Her father, the strong farmer,
Had horses, sheep and cows,
One hundred verdant acres
And slates upon his house.

And she stole with the starlight
From where her life began
To roam the roads of Ireland
With a travelling tinker man.

His hair was brown and curling,
His eyes were brown as well,
His tongue would charm the hinges
Off the gates of hell.

At Caher fair she saw him
As she was hurrying by,
And the song that he was singing
Would lure lark from the sky.

Her footsteps slowed to standing,
She stood and stared that day;
He made a noose of music
And pulled her heart away.

And so she left her slate-roof
And her father rich and strong
Because her mind was turning
About a tinker's song.

They walked the roads of Ireland,
Went up the hills and down,
Passed many an empty bogland,
Through many a noisy town.

She rode upon the ass-cart
To rest a tired leg,
She learned the lore of tinkers,
And he taught her how to beg.

"The tree-tied house of planter
Is colder than east wind,
The hall-door of the gombeen
Has no welcome for our kind.

"The farmstead of the grabber
Is hungry as a stone,
But the little homes of Kerry
Will give us half their own."

She cut the cards for girls
And made their eyes glow bright,
She read the palms of women
And saw their lips go tight.

"A dark man will marry you
On a day of June;
There's money across water
Coming to you soon.

"Oh, he'll be rich and handsome
And I see a bridal feast;
Your daughter will dwell in Dublin,
Your son will be a priest."

They rode along together,
The woman pale and wan,
The black ass young and giddy,
And the brown-eyed tinker man.

He bought up mules and jennets
And sang songs far and wide;
But she never gave him children
To fill his heart with pride.

She never gave him children
To spoil his sleep with cries,
But she saw his empty arms
And the hunger in his eyes.

She saw the lonely bogland,
She felt the killing wind,
And the fine home of her father
Kept turning in her mind.

She felt the chill rain falling,
She grew tired of it all,
And twisting in the darkness
She died within her shawl.

They dug a cold grave for her
And left her all alone,
And the tinker man went with them,
His heart as grey as stone.

"She was the best of women,
The flower of the ball,
She never gave me children
But that's no blame at all.

"A lass may break her mother's heart,
A son his father's head:
Maybe she is happier now
Sleeping with the dead."

He drank his fill of porter
And turned his face to life,
And hit the road for Puck Fair
To get another wife.

THE POTATO DIGGERS by Paul Henry.
1912. Oil on canvas.
The National Gallery of Ireland, Dublin

SPRAYING THE POTATOES

PATRICK KAVANAGH (1904–1967)

The barrels of blue potato-spray
Stood on a headland of July
Beside an orchard wall where roses
Were young girls hanging from the sky.

The flocks of green potato-stalks
Were blossom spread for sudden flight,
The Kerr's Pinks in a frivelled blue,
The Arran Banners wearing white.

And over that potato-field
A hazy veil of woven sun.
Dandelions growing on headlands, showing
Their unloved hearts to everyone.

And I was there with the knapsack sprayer
On the barrel's edge poised. A wasp was floating
Dead on a sunken briar leaf
Over a copper-poisoned ocean.

The axle-roll of a rut-locked cart
Broke the burnt stick of noon in two.
An old man came through a cornfield
Remembering his youth and some Ruth he knew.

He turned my way. "God further the work."
He echoed an ancient farming prayer.
I thanked him. He eyed the potato-drills.
He said: "You are bound to have good ones there."

We talked and our talk was a theme of kings,
A theme for strings. He hunkered down
In the shade of the orchard wall. O roses
The old man dies in the young girl's frown.

And poet lost to potato-fields,
Remembering the lime and copper smell
Of the spraying barrels he is not lost
Or till blossomed stalks cannot weave a spell.

TO THE BLACKSMITH WITH A SPADE

OWEN ROE O'SULLIVAN (1748–1784)

Make me a handle as straight as the mast of a ship,
    Seumas you clever man, witty and bountiful,
Sprung through the Geraldine lords from the kings of Greece,
    And fix the treadle and send it back to me soon.

Because the spade is the only thing keeping me now—
    And you know that my thirst for knowledge was always deep.
I'll shoulder my traps and make for Galway that night
    To a place where I'm sure of sixpence a day and my keep.

And whenever I'm feeling low at the end of the day,
    And the ganger comes round and assures me I'm dodging it well,
I'll drop a few words about Death's adventurous way
    And the wars of the Greeks in Troy, and the kings that fell.

I'll speak of Samson who had great strength and pride,
    And Alexander, the man who was first of men,
And Caesar who took the sway on the Roman side
    And maybe I'll speak of the feats of Achilles then.

Explaining of course how it came to MacTrain to die,
    And Deirdre the beauty who put the whole world astray,
And he'll listen and gawk, and not notice an hour go by,
    And so my learning will lift me through the day.

They'll give me my pay in a lump when the harvest's done,
    I'll tuck it away in a knot in my shirt to keep,
And back to the village, singing and mad for fun—
    And I promise I won't spend sixpence until we meet.

For you're a man like myself with an antique thirst,
    So need I say how we'll give the story an end?
We'll shout and rattle our cans the livelong night
    Till there isn't as much as the price of a pint to spend.

Between the mud bed sown with bronze daggers and gold
                                                    fibulae

And the craning reeds guarded by ornamental herons

The pike in his cell

THE GREAT IRISH PIKE I and II by Barrie Cooke. 1982. Lithographs. Collection of An Chomhairle Ealaíon/The Arts Council, Ireland

The Great Irish Pike

The pike has been condemned.
The Wyrm, dipping his lily in the lake, decreed it
This is no place for anything fishy
That revives the smile of the Dragon.

He fell asleep in Job.
He woke in the Book of Venom

And in the Court of Beauty-Care and Cosmetics
His features are established as the criminal norm.
No trial for those eyes. No appeal
For that mouth. And flesh of such length
So gilled and slimed, is flagrante delicto.

Nursery Trout bore witness in falsetto.
Shameless hatchery smolts
United themselves with the helpless and oppressed.
And the portly rudd
Winsomely cast themselves as the allotted
Mediaeval maidens.

Whenever the pike tried to protest
The show of his fangs emptied the hearing.

Therefore the vibrato of Sunday bells
Atomised him
In the straitened souls of our grandmothers

The water-colourist of human progress
Is painting the ponds afresh,
The princes and the nymphs, without him.

Even the deft snake of Freud
Invested him, religiously,
For nightmare returns only——

Can he still be said to exist?

Between the mud bed sown with bronze dapples and gold fibulae
And the crannog reeds guarded by ornamental lesions
The pike in his cell

Only survives Till the hired German beheads him

And strings his skull, with Twelve others,
Along the gunnel of his Shannon cruiser

Or nails it on a plaque
Over the resurrection of Valhalla.

                                        Ted Hughes

Included is a poem by Ted Hughes, the British Poet Laureate.

Field-girdling fences of unmortared stone in Aran. Photograph by Jill Uris

LAUNCHING THE CURRAGH by Paul Henry. Early 20th century. Oil on canvas. The National Gallery of Ireland, Dublin

Man of Aran. Photograph by Jill Uris

IRISH SWEATERS

SHIRLEY GRAVES COCHRANE (BORN 1939)

"Ladies and gentlemen—
the sweaters of old Ireland!"
and down the runway come
Maeve and Erin and the other Dublin models
hips switching, eyes scorning
and Maurice, sheepish in his cowl.
"Each household had its special pattern—
you could tell a family sweater anywhere."

Aye—even at the bottom of the sea;
for grannies knit the shrouds of grandson
fishermen who never learned to swim
(to keep the agony of drowning short).
And long after the eyes were gone
and fish explored the geography of skull
the sweaters held and told us who they were—
Cormac and Tom and even Donovan.

See how the stitches knit the bones together.

ACHILL HORSES by Mainie Jellett. 1944. Oil on canvas. The National Gallery of Ireland, Dublin

BEFORE THE START by Jack B. Yeats.
1915. Oil on canvas.
The National Gallery of Ireland, Dublin

AT GALWAY RACES

W. B. YEATS (1865–1939)

There where the course is,
Delight makes all of the one mind,
The riders upon the galloping horses,
The crowd that closes in behind:
We, too, had good attendance once,
Hearers and hearteners of the work;
Aye, horsemen for companions,
Before the merchant and the clerk
Breathed on the world with timid breath.
Sing on: somewhere at some new moon,
We'll learn that sleeping is not death,
Hearing the whole earth change its tune,
Its flesh being wild, and it again
Crying aloud as the racecourse is,
And we find hearteners among men
That ride upon horses.

I AM OF IRELAND
ANONYMOUS (EARLY ENGLISH)

Icham of Irlaunde
Ant of the holy londe of irlonde
Gode sir pray ich ye
for of saynte charite,
come ant daunce wyt me,
in irlaunde.

"I AM OF IRELAND"

W. B. YEATS (1865-1939)

"I am of Ireland,
And the Holy Land of Ireland,
And time runs on," cried she.
"Come out of charity,
Come dance with me in Ireland."

One man, one man alone
In that outlandish gear,
One solitary man
Of all that rambled there
Had turned his stately head.
"That is a long way off,
And time runs on," he said,
"And the night grows rough."

"I am of Ireland,
And the Holy Land of Ireland,
And time runs on," cried she.
"Come out of charity
And dance with me in Ireland."

"The fiddlers are all thumbs,
Or the fiddle-string accursed,
The drums and the kettledrums
And the trumpets all are burst,
And the trombone," cried he,
"The trumpet and trombone,"
And cocked a malicious eye,
"But time runs on, runs on."

"I am of Ireland,
And the Holy Land of Ireland,
And time runs on," cried she.
"Come out of charity
And dance with me in Ireland."

DARK ROSALEEN

TRANSLATED FROM THE IRISH (C. 19TH CENTURY) BY JAMES CLARENCE MANGAN (1803–1849)

O my Dark Rosaleen,
  Do not sigh, do not weep!
The priests are on the ocean green,
  They march along the Deep.
There's wine . . . from the royal Pope
  Upon the ocean green;
And Spanish ale shall give you hope,
  My Dark Rosaleen!
  My own Rosaleen!
Shall glad your heart, shall give you hope,
Shall give you health, and help, and hope,
  My Dark Rosaleen.

Over hills and through dales,
  Have I roamed for your sake;
All yesterday I sailed with sails
  On river and on lake.
The Erne . . . at its highest flood
  I dashed across unseen,
For there was lightning in my blood,
  My Dark Rosaleen!
  My own Rosaleen!
Oh! there was lightning in my blood,
Red lightning lightened through my blood,
  My Dark Rosaleen!

All day long in unrest
  To and fro do I move,
The very soul within my breast
  Is wasted for you, love!
The heart . . . in my bosom faints
  To think of you, my Queen,
My life of life, my saint of saints,
  My Dark Rosaleen!
  My own Rosaleen!
To hear your sweet and sad complaints,
My life, my love, my saint of saints,
  My Dark Rosaleen!

Woe and pain, pain and woe,
  Are my lot night and noon,
To see your bright face clouded so,
  Like to the mournful moon.
But yet . . . will I rear your throne
  Again in golden sheen;
'Tis you shall reign, shall reign alone,
  My Dark Rosaleen!
  My own Rosaleen!
'Tis you shall have the golden throne,
'Tis you shall reign, and reign alone,
  My Dark Rosaleen!

Over dews, over sands
  Will I fly for your weal;
Your holy delicate white hands
  Shall girdle me with steel.
At home . . . in your emerald bowers,
  From morning's dawn till e'en,
You'll pray for me, my flower of flowers,
  My Dark Rosaleen!
  My fond Rosaleen!
You'll think of me through daylight's hours,
My virgin flower, my flower of flowers,
  My Dark Rosaleen!

I could scale the blue air,
  I could plough the high hills,
Oh, I could kneel all night in prayer,
  To heal your many ills!
And one . . . beamy smile from you
  Would float like light between
My toils and me, my own, my true,
  My Dark Rosaleen!
  My fond Rosaleen!
Would give me life and soul anew,
A second life, a soul anew,
  My Dark Rosaleen!

EARTH MOTHER by Joan Walsh-Smith. 1981. Fiberglass

A large sculpture temporarily installed in a field.

THE MUSE OF AMERGIN

TRANSLATED FROM THE EARLY IRISH BY JOHN MONTAGUE (BORN 1929)

I speak for Erin,
Sailed and fertile sea,
Fertile fruitful mountains,
Fruitful moist woods,
Moist overflowing lochs,
Flowing hillside springs,
Springs of men assembling,
Assembling men at Tara,
Tara, hill of tribes,
Tribes of the sons of Mil,
Mil of boats and ships,
The high ship of Éire,
Éire of high recital,
Recital skilfully done,
The skill of the women
Of Breisi, of Buagnai;
That haughty lady, Éire,
By Eremon conquered,
Ir and Eber bespoken:
I speak for Erin.

KATHALEEN NY-HOULAHAN

TRANSLATED FROM THE IRISH (18TH CENTURY) BY JAMES CLARENCE MANGAN (1803–1849)

Long they pine in weary woe, the nobles of our land,
Long they wander to and fro, proscribed, alas! and banned;
Feastless, houseless, altarless, they bear the exile's brand;
    But their hope is in the coming-to of Kathaleen Ny-Houlahan!

Think her not a ghastly hag, too hideous to be seen,
Call her not unseemly names, our matchless Kathaleen;
Young she is, and fair she is, and would be crowned queen,
    Were the king's son at home here with Kathaleen Ny-Houlahan!

Sweet and mild would look her face, O none so sweet and mild,
Could she crush the foes by whom her beauty is reviled;
Woollen plaids would grace herself, and robes of silk her child,
    If the king's son were living here with Kathaleen Ny-Houlahan!

Sore disgrace it is to see the Arbitress of thrones,
Vassal to a *Saxoneen* of cold and sapless bones!
Bitter anguish wrings our souls—with heavy sighs and groans
    We wait the young Deliverer of Kathaleen Ny-Houlahan!

Let us pray to Him who holds life's issues in His hands—
Him who formed the mighty globe, with all its thousand lands;
Girdling them with seas and mountains, rivers deep, and strands,
    To cast a look of pity upon Kathaleen Ny-Houlahan!

He who over sands and waves led Israel along—
He who fed, with heavenly bread, that chosen tribe and throng—
He who stood by Moses, when his foes were fierce and strong—
    May He show forth His might in saving Kathaleen Ny-Houlahan!

LADY LAVERY AS KATHLEEN NI HOULIHAN
by Sir John Lavery. 1923. Oil on canvas.
Courtesy of The Central Bank of Ireland, Dublin

This image was used on Irish currency.

RED HANRAHAN'S SONG ABOUT IRELAND
W. B. YEATS (1865–1939)

The old brown thorn-trees break in two high over Cummen Strand,
Under a bitter black wind that blows from the left hand;
Our courage breaks like an old tree in a black wind and dies,
But we have hidden in our hearts the flame out of the eyes
Of Cathleen, the daughter of Houlihan.

The wind has bundled up the clouds high over Knocknarea,
And thrown the thunder on the stones for all that Maeve can say.
Angers that are like noisy clouds have set our hearts abeat;
But we have all bent low and low and kissed the quiet feet
Of Cathleen, the daughter of Houlihan.

The yellow pool has overflowed high up on Clooth-na-Bare,
For the wet winds are blowing out of the clinging air;
Like heavy flooded waters our bodies and our blood;
But purer than a tall candle before the Holy Rood
Is Cathleen, the daughter of Houlihan.

UNKNOWN IDEAL

DORA SIGERSON (1866 – 1918)

Whose is the voice that will not let me rest?
I hear it speak.
Where is the shore will gratify my quest,
Show what I seek?
Not yours, weak Muse, to mimic that far voice,
With halting tongue;
No peace, sweet land, to bid my heart rejoice
Your groves among.

Whose is the loveliness I know is by,
Yet cannot place?
Is it perfection of the sea or sky,
Or human face?

Not yours, my pencil, to delineate
The splendid smile!
Blind in the sun, we struggle on with Fate
That glows the while.

Whose are the feet that pass me, echoing
On unknown ways?
Whose are the lips that only part to sing
Through all my days?
Not yours, fond youth, to fill mine eager eyes
That still adore
Beauty that tarries not, nor satisfies
For evermore.

MOLLY MACREE by Sir Thomas Alfred Jones.
Mid-19th century. Gouache with varnish on paper.
The National Gallery of Ireland, Dublin

BRIGHTNESS OF BRIGHTNESS

EGAN O RAHILLY (1670–1728)

TRANSLATED FROM THE IRISH BY FRANK O'CONNOR (1903–1966)

Brightness of brightness lonely met me where I wandered,
  Crystal of crystal only by her eyes were splendid,
Sweetness of sweetness lightly in her speech she squandered,
  Rose-red and lily-glow brightly in her cheeks contended.

Ringlet on ringlet flowed tress on tress of yellow flaming
  Hair, and swept the dew that glowed on the grass in showers behind her,
Vesture her breasts bore, mirror-bright, oh, mirror-shaming
  That her fairy northern land yielded her from birth to bind them.

There she told me, told me as one that might in loving languish,
  Told me of his coming, he for whom the crown was wreathed.
Told me of their ruin who banished him to utter anguish,
  More too she told me I dare not in my song have breathed.

Frenzy of frenzy 'twas that her beauty did not numb me,
  That I neared the royal serf, the vassal queen that held me vassal,
Then I called on Mary's Son to shield me, she started from me,
  And she fled, the lady, a lightning flash to Luachra Castle.

Fleetly too I fled in wild flight with body trembling
  Over reefs of rock and sand, bog and shining plain and strand, sure
That my feet would find a path to that place of sad assembling,
  House of houses reared of old in cold dark druid grandeur.

There a throng of wild creatures mocked me with elfin laughter,
  And a group of mild maidens, tall with twining silken tresses,
Bound in bitter bonds they laid me there, and a moment after
  See my lady laughing share a pot-bellied clown's caresses.

Truth of truth I told her in grief that it shamed her
  To see her with a sleek foreign mercenary lover
When the highest peak of Scotland's race already thrice had named her,
  And waited in longing for his exile to be over.

When she heard me speak, she wept, but she wept for pride,
  And tears flowed down in streams from cheeks so bright and comely,
She sent a watchman with me to lead me to the mountainside—
  Brightness of brightness who met me walking lonely.

IRELAND

JOHN HEWITT (BORN 1907)

We Irish pride ourselves as patriots
and tell the beadroll of the valiant ones
since Clontarf's sunset saw the Norsemen broken . . .
Aye, and before that too we had our heroes:
but they were mighty fighters and victorious.
The later men got nothing save defeat,
hard transatlantic sidewalks or the scaffold . . .

We Irish, vainer than tense Lucifer,
are yet content with half-a-dozen turf,
and cry our adoration for a bog,
rejoicing in the rain that never ceases,
and happy to stride over the sterile acres,
or stony hills that scarcely feed a sheep.
But we are fools, I say, are ignorant fools
to waste the spirit's warmth in this cold air,
to spend our wit and love and poetry
on half-a-dozen peat and a black bog.

We are not native here or anywhere.
We were the keltic wave that broke over Europe,
and ran up this bleak beach among these stones:
but when the tide ebbed, were left stranded here
in crevices, and ledge-protected pools
that have grown salter with the drying up
of the great common flow that kept us sweet
with fresh cold draughts from deep down in the ocean.

So we are bitter, and are dying out
in terrible harshness in this lonely place,
and what we think is love for usual rock,
or old affection for our customary ledge,
is but forgotten longing for the sea
that cries far out and calls us to partake
in his great tidal movements round the earth.

THE INSULAR CELTS

CIARAN CARSON (BORN 1948)

Having left hard ground behind
in the hardness of their place-names,
they have sailed out for an island:

as along the top of a wood
their boats have crossed the green ridges,
so has the pale sky overhead

appeared as a milky surface,
a white plain where the speckled fish
drift in lamb-white clouds of fleece.

As their sails will be covering
for the first houses that they build,
so their boats will be hovering

in the smoke of their first fires,
like red blood falling will be
their landing on the first shores.

They will come back to the warm earth
and call it by possessive names:
mother, thorned rose, woman, love's birth;

to hard hills of stone they will give
the words for breast; to meadowland,
the soft gutturals of rivers,

tongues of water; to firm plains, flesh,
as one day we will discover
their way of living, in their death.

They entered their soft beds of soil
not as graves, for this was the land
that they had fought for, loved, and killed

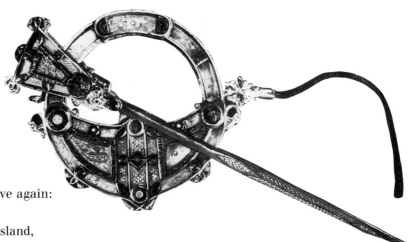

each other for. They'd arrive again:
death could be no horizon
but the shoreline of their island,

a coming and going as flood
comes after ebb. In the spirals
of their brooches is seen the flight

of one thing into the other:
as the wheel-ruts on a battle-
plain have filled with silver water,

the confused circles of their wars,
their cattle-raids, have worked themselves
to a laced pattern of old scars.

In their speckled parchments we read
of word-play in the halls of kings,
of how these people loved to fight,

yet where are their fine houses now?
They are hammered into the ground,
they have been laid bare by the plough.

Yet their death, since it is no real
death, will happen over again
and again, their bones will seem still

to fall in the hail beneath hooves
of horses, their limbs will drift down
as the branches that trees have loosed.

We cannot yet say why or how
they could not take things as they were.
Some day we will learn of how

their bronze swords took the shape of leaves;
their gold spears are found in cornfields,
their arrows are found in trees.

TARA BROOCH.
8th century A.D.
Gilt silver,
amber, glass, enamel,
and gold filigree.
National Museum of Ireland,
Dublin

HEAD OF A YOUNG CELTIC MAN.
1st century A.D. Bronze.
Bernisches Historisches Museum,
Bern

FOR PADDY MAC

PADRAIC FALLON (1905–1974)

I

Once, so long ago,
You used to probe me gently for the lost
Country, sensing somehow in my airs
The vivid longlipped peasantry of
Last century

And those bronze men pushed
With their diminishing herds far out on
The last ledge of original earth,
Fomorian types
In the big one-eyed sky

All messed up with sundogs and
Too many rainbows, and that wishwashing
   head of Bran
In the toppling arches seaward sailing and singing
On his weathered maypole from
A caved-in skull.

Ours were the metres
Of early waters, the first argosy hardly home
With new women, orgies
When the moon rode round
Stone circles counting her twelve.

Homer's people.
And wasn't I lucky, born with
Boundaries floating, language still making
Out of the broadlands where my fathers
Tended their clouds of ewes?

Bunkum, Dear P. The thing was gone, or
Never was. And we were the leftovers,
Lord-ridden and pulpit-thumped for all our wild
Cudgels of Gaelic. Ours was Lever's
One-horse country; the bailiff at the bighouse door.

And hags hung all day
In turfsmoke among the fowl where I was licked.
That was a town
Walled and towered as Troy, and never sieged
   for a woman:
Trading bullocks and pennies for glory gone;

And watched from the top of a shilling the homespun
   fellows
Selling their spades on hiring days,
For a year and a day the dear flesh off their bones
From penury to slavery,
The soul thrown in for a spare.

That was my country, beast, sky and anger:
For music a mad piper in the mud;
No poets I knew of; or they mouthed each other's words;
Such low powered gods
They died, as they were born, in byres.

Oh, maybe some rags and tatters did sing.
But poetry, for all your talk, is never that simple,
Coming out of a stone ditch in the broadlands
Newborn, or from
The fitful pibroch of a lonely thorn,

Or old saws at winter fires.
Muted the big words. Love was left
To eloping earls or such
Lest the snake creep up, usurping the ancient timber
And some odd bloom come bursting from the Cross.

II

And you speak of Raftery, that bold tongue, the tramp
In borrowed bootleather, those rainy eyes
Lifted to empty heaven from a blind man's stick;
I sang like him you say, and praised women,
And I had the true cow's lick;

You who should know how every poet must
Baptize first the font and the very waters,
And have no godfathers but this great thirst
For what is not;
And no mothers;

Who must quote Ambrose crookedly (Nam quid divinius
Isto ut puncto exiguo culpa cadet
Populi), bog Latin for
The bit of earth we tread
Into metaphor

Knowing we're just another civilisation
To be dumped, but go on, say it you,
We've eaten all the Gods yet bow the knee,
And are only really at home
In the larger toleration of the poem.

Carefully, now that you are dead,
I must amend the scribbles of the tribe
Lest sheepman and bullhead
Become a frieze of fathers like stone man,
Hieratic, almost Egyptian,

And from the uncreated, with arms widespread,
From puncto exiguo, beyond the dead
And Lazarus rising, where God is making still
Release the flood
Of living images for good and ill.

Dear P. I'll never know
What you brought over and passed on,
But this seems certain as I grow:
Man lives; Gods die:
It is only the genuflection that survives.

Donkey auction, Co. Kerry.
Photograph by Richard Fitzgerald

RUNE

MICHAEL LONGLEY (BORN 1939)

Poems in the palm of the hand, life-lines,
Fingers tapping the ridge of the shin-bone,
The bridge of the nose, fingerprints, breath;
Then the silvery skin of the lifeless,
Ivy increasing the secrets, the answers—
The physician's power in cold dwellings,
Candles behind this veil of synonyms,
A blind man's lovely wife and signature.

The Dunloe Ogham Stone, Co. Kerry.
Photograph: Commissioners of Public Works, Ireland

THE DOWNFALL OF HEATHENDOM
TRANSLATED FROM THE IRISH (C. 9TH CENTURY) BY FRANK O'CONNOR (1903–1966)

Ailill the king is vanished.
    Vanished Croghan's fort,
Kings to Clonmacnois
    Come to pay their court.

In quiet Clonmacnois
    About Saint Kieran's feet
Everlasting quires
    Raise a concert sweet.

Allen and its lords
    Both are overthrown,
Brigid's house is full,
    Far her fame has flown.

Navan town is shattered,
    Ruins everywhere;
Glendalough remains,
    Half a world is there.

Ferns is a blazing torch,
    Ferns is great and good,
But Beg, son of Owen,
    And his proud hosts are dead.

Old haunts of the heathen
    Filled from ancient days
Are but deserts now
    Where no pilgrim prays.

Little places taken
    First by twos and threes
Are like Rome reborn,
    Peopled sanctuaries.

Heathendom has gone down
    Though it was everywhere;
God the Father's kingdom
    Fills heaven and earth and air.

Sing the kings defeated!
    Sing the Donals down!
Clonmacnois triumphant,
    Cronan with the crown.

All the hills of evil,
    Level now they lie;
All the quiet valleys
    Tossed up to the sky.

Early Iron Age stone idol from Beltany, Co. Donegal. National Museum of Ireland, Dublin

THE OPEN DOOR
TRANSLATED FROM THE EARLY IRISH BY FRANK O'CONNOR (1903–1966)

King of stars,
    Dark or bright my house may be,
But I close my door on none
    Lest Christ close his door on me.

THE CRUCIFIXION.
8th century A.D.
Gilt bronze plaque.
National Museum of Ireland, Dublin

THE BOOK OF KELLS

PADRAIC COLUM (1881–1972)

First, make a letter like a monument—
An upright like the fast-held hewn stone
Immovable, and half-rimming it
The strength of Behemoth his neck-bone,
And underneath that yoke, a staff, a rood
Of no less hardness than the cedar wood.

Then, on a page made golden as the crown
Of sainted man, a scripture you enscroll
Blackly, firmly, with the quickened skill
Lessoned by famous masters in our school,
And with an ink whose lustre will keep fresh
For fifty generations of our flesh.

And limn below it the Evangelist
In raddled coat, on bench abidingly,
Simple and bland: Matthew his name or Mark,
Or Luke or John; the book is by his knee,
And thereby its similitudes: Lion,
Or Calf, or Eagle, or Exalted Man.

The winds that blow around the world—the four
Winds in their colours on your pages join—
The Northern Wind—its blackness interpose;
The Southern Wind—its blueness gather in;
In redness and in greenness manifest
The splendours of the Winds of East and West.

And with these colours on a ground of gold
Compose a circuit will be seen by men
As endless patience, but is nether web
Of endless effort—a strict pattern:
Illumination lighting interlace
Of cirque and scroll, of panel and lattice.

A single line describes them and enfolds,
One line, one course where term there is none,
Which in its termlessness is envoying
The going forth and the return one.
With man and beast and bird and fish therein
Transformed to species that have never been.

With mouth a-gape or beak a-gape each stands
Initial to a verse of miracle,
Of mystery and of marvel (Depth of God!)
That Alpha or Omega may not spell,
Then finished with these wonders and these signs,
Turn to the figures of your first outlines.

Axal, our angel, has sustained you so
In hand, in brain; now to him seal that thing
With figures many as the days of man,
And colours, like the fire's enamelling—
That baulk, that letter you have greatly reared
To stay the violence of the entering Word!

SAINT MATTHEW.
Illuminated manuscript page from
THE BOOK OF KELLS.
Late 8th–9th century A.D.
Courtesy The Board of Trinity
College, Dublin

THE HERMITAGE

TRANSLATED FROM THE IRISH (C. 9TH CENTURY)
BY FRANK O'CONNOR (1903–1966)

Grant me sweet Christ the grace to find—
    Son of the living God!—
A small hut in a lonesome spot
    To make it my abode.

A little pool but very clear
    To stand beside the place
Where all men's sins are washed away
    By sanctifying grace.

A pleasant woodland all about
    To shield it from the wind,
And make a home for singing birds
    Before it and behind.

A southern aspect for the heat,
    A stream along its foot,
A smooth green lawn with rich top soil
    Propitious to all fruit.

My choice of men to live with me
    And pray to God as well;
Quiet men of humble mind—
    Their number I shall tell.

Four files of three or three of four
    To give the psalter forth;
Six to pray by the south church wall
    And six along the north.

Two by two my dozen friends—
    To tell the number right—
Praying with me to move the King
    Who gives the sun its light.

A lovely church, a home for God,
    Bedecked with linen fine,
Where over the white Gospel page
    The Gospel candles shine.

A little house where all may dwell
    And body's care be sought,
Where none shows lust or arrogance,
    None thinks an evil thought.

And all I ask for housekeeping
    I get and pay no fees,
Leeks from the garden, poultry, game,
    Salmon and trout and bees.

My share of clothing and of food
    From the King of fairest face,
And I to sit at times alone
    And pray in every place.

Remains of early monastic structures, Skellig Islands, Co. Kerry.
Photograph by Kathleen Jo Ryan

Wooden cross.
Late 17th–mid-18th century.
National Museum of Ireland, Dublin

*The simplicity of this small wooden cross reflects
the difficult position of the Catholic church during
the Penal Law period.*

ADVENT

PATRICK KAVANAGH (1906–1967)

We have tested and tasted too much, lover—
Through a chink too wide there comes in no wonder.
But here in the Advent-darkened room
Where the dry black bread and the sugarless tea
Of penance will charm back the luxury
Of a child's soul, we'll return to Doom
The knowledge we stole but could not use.

And the newness that was in every stale thing
When we looked at it as children: the spirit-shocking
Wonder in a black slanting Ulster hill
Or the prophetic astonishment in the tedious talking
Of an old fool will awake for us and bring
You and me to the yard gate to watch the whins
And the bog-holes, cart-tracks, old stables where Time begins.

O after Christmas we'll have no need to go searching
For the difference that sets an old phrase burning—
We'll hear it in the whispered argument of a churning
Or in the streets where the village boys are lurching.
And we'll hear it among decent men too
Who barrow dung in gardens under trees,
Wherever life pours ordinary plenty.
Won't we be rich, my love and I, and please
God we shall not ask for reason's payment,
The why of heart-breaking strangeness in dreeping hedges
Nor analyse God's breath in common statement.
We have thrown into the dust-bin the clay-minted wages
Of pleasure, knowledge and the conscious hour—
And Christ comes with a January flower.

THE NAMELESS ONE

JAMES CLARENCE MANGAN (1803 – 1849)

Roll forth, my song, like the rushing river,
   That sweeps along to the mighty sea;
God will inspire me while I deliver
     My soul of thee!

Tell thou the world, when my bones lie whitening
   Amid the last homes of youth and eld,
That there was once one whose veins ran lightning
     No eye beheld.

Tell how his boyhood was one drear night-hour,
   How shone for *him*, through his griefs and gloom,
No star of all heaven sends to light our
     Path to the tomb.

Roll on, my song, and to after ages
   Tell how, disdaining all earth can give,
He would have taught men, from wisdom's pages,
     The way to live.

And tell how trampled, derided, hated,
   And worn by weakness, disease, and wrong,
He fled for shelter to God, who mated
     His soul with song—

With song which alway, sublime or vapid,
   Flowed like a rill in the morning beam,
Perchance not deep, but intense and rapid—
     A mountain stream.

Tell how this Nameless, condemned for years long
   To herd with demons from hell beneath,
Saw things that made him, with groans and tears, long
     For even death.

Go on to tell how, with genius wasted,
   Betrayed in friendship, befooled in love,
With spirit shipwrecked, and young hopes blasted,
     He still, still strove.

Till, spent with toil, dreeing death for others,
   And some whose hands should have wrought for *him*
(If children live not for sires and mothers),
     His mind grew dim.

And he fell far through that pit abysmal
   The gulf and grave of Maginn and Burns,
And pawned his soul for the devil's dismal
     Stock of returns.

But yet redeemed it in days of darkness,
   And shapes and signs of the final wrath,
When death, in hideous and ghastly starkness,
     Stood on his path.

And tell how now, amid wreck and sorrow,
   And want, and sickness, and houseless nights,
He bides in calmness the silent morrow,
     That no ray lights.

And lives he still, then? Yes! Old and hoary
   At thirty-nine, from despair and woe,
He lives enduring what future story
     Will never know.

Him grant a grave to, ye pitying noble,
   Deep in your bosoms! There let him dwell!
He, too, had tears for all souls in trouble,
     Here and in hell.

THE MEETING OF SAINT BRENDAN WITH THE UNHAPPY JUDAS
by Harry Clarke. Early 20th century. Stained-glass panel acided, stained, and painted.
Crawford Municipal Art Gallery, Cork

DOCKER

SEAMUS HEANEY (BORN 1939)

There, in the corner, staring at his drink.
The cap juts like a gantry's crossbeam,
Cowling plated forehead and sledgehead jaw.
Speech is clamped in the lips' vice.

That fist would drop a hammer on a Catholic—
Oh yes, that kind of thing could start again;
The only Roman collar he tolerates
Smiles all round his sleek pint of porter.

Mosaic imperatives bang home like rivets;
God is a foreman with certain definite views
Who orders life in shifts of work and leisure.
A factory horn will blare the Resurrection.

He sits, strong and blunt as a Celtic cross,
Clearly used to silence and an armchair:
Tonight the wife and children will be quiet
At slammed door and smoker's cough in the hall.

The Cross of Muiredach, Monasterboice, Co. Louth.
West face, showing the Crucifixion. c. A.D. 920.
Photograph: Commissioners of Public Works, Ireland

ST. DOULAGH'S CHURCH—1813.
Lithograph.
Collection Charles Sullivan

ROBERT SAT

TOM MATTHEWS (BORN 1945)

The congregation was scandalised
When Robert sat in his pew and read a paperback

My mother said afterwards
"If he wasn't interested why did he come"

And I marvelled at her
For she never thought of applying that criterion to me

And I marvelled at Robert too
Able to read so calmly in the midst of so much hate

Robert is now doing very nicely thank you
He emigrated to Canada
And broke both legs in a skiing accident
And married a nurse

LETTER TO DEREK MAHON

MICHAEL LONGLEY (BORN 1939)

And did we come into our own
When, minus muse and lexicon,
We traced in August sixty-nine
Our imaginary Peace Line
Around the burnt-out houses of
The Catholics we'd scarcely loved,
Two Sisyphuses come to budge
The sticks and stones of an old grudge,

Two poetic conservatives
In the city of guns and long knives,
Our ears receiving then and there
The stereophonic nightmare
Of the Shankill and the Falls,
Our matches struck on crumbling walls
To light us as we moved at last
Through the back alleys of Belfast?

Why it mattered to have you here
You who journeyed to Inishere
With me, years back, one Easter when
With MacIntyre and the lone Dane
Our footsteps lifted up the larks,
Echoing off those western rocks
And down that darkening arcade
Hung with the failures of our trade,

Will understand. We were tongue-tied
Companions of the island's dead
In the graveyard among the dunes,
Eavesdroppers on conversations
With a Jesus who spoke Irish—
We were strangers in that parish,
Black tea with bacon and cabbage
For our sacraments and pottage,

Dank blankets making up our Lent
Till, islanders ourselves, we bent
Our knees and cut the watery sod
From the lazy-bed where slept a God
We couldn't count among our friends,
Although we'd taken in our hands
Splinters of driftwood nailed and stuck
On the rim of the Atlantic.

Irish stone fort in Aran.
Photograph by Jill Uris

*This fort is estimated to be
several thousand years old.*

THE VIKING TERROR
TRANSLATED FROM THE EARLY IRISH BY FRANK O'CONNOR (1903–1966)

Since tonight the wind is high,
The sea's white mane a fury
I need not fear the hordes of Hell
Coursing the Irish Channel.

THE MEETING OF THOMAS, EARL OF GLOUCESTER, AND ART MACMURROUGH. From JEAN CRETON'S CHRONICLE. c. 1401–05. The British Library, London

One of the many invasions of Ireland.

THE KING OF CONNACHT
TRANSLATED FROM THE EARLY IRISH BY FRANK O'CONNOR (1903–1966)

"Have you seen Hugh,
The Connacht king in the field?"
"All that we saw
Was his shadow under his shield."

As rom ṅ Illa bune read mǝzlṅṅ ṅ̃ er aaī ṁ mcꝺoꝛ ēuꝗ t̃ ꝛ ꝫ
ꝺa ꝺoca fꝫ a ꝫ e ar mo   fuꝗ n ꝺolc a coꝛ naꝺ aꝺ uꝑꝗ
fꝫ   ꝺa ca ꝺeꝫ ṅꝛꝫ a mꝺa ꝛ ꝑ tꝛꝫ ꝣ e fꝫ ꝛ a cꝺaꝺ
reacht ṁa ꝺṁaṅa ꝛ ꝫ bꝫ ꝫ atꝛ   ṅꝺ ꝺo ꝛe naꝣ ṁ ꝫ

THE MARRIAGE OF PRINCESS AOIFE (EVA) AND THE EARL OF PEMBROKE (STRONGBOW)
by Daniel Maclise. Mid-19th century. Watercolor on paper.
The National Gallery of Ireland, Dublin

A symbolic union of Irish and Norman dynasties.

HOPE
TRANSLATED FROM THE IRISH (C. 17TH–18TH CENTURY)
BY FRANK O'CONNOR (1903–1966)

Life has conquered, the wind has blown away
Alexander, Caesar and all their power and sway;
Tara and Troy have made no longer stay—
Maybe the English too will have their day.

HISTORY AND GENEALOGY OF THE DE BURGO FAMILY
by Seaán Mac William Burke. 16th-century manuscript.
Courtesy The Board of Trinity College, Dublin

DEIRDRE'S LAMENT FOR THE SONS OF USNACH

TRANSLATED FROM THE EARLY IRISH BY SIR SAMUEL FERGUSON (1810–1886)

The lions of the hill are gone,
And I am left alone—alone—
Dig the grave both wide and deep,
For I am sick, and fain would sleep!

The falcons of the wood are flown,
And I am left alone—alone—
Dig the grave both deep and wide,
And let us slumber side by side.

The dragons of the rock are sleeping,
Sleep that wakes not for our weeping:
Dig the grave and make it ready;
Lay me on my true Love's body.

Lay their spears and bucklers bright
By the warriors' sides aright;
Many a day the Three before me
On their linkèd bucklers bore me.

Lay upon the low grave floor,
'Neath each head, the blue claymore;
Many a time the noble Three
Redden'd those blue blades for me.

Lay the collars, as is meet,
Of their greyhounds at their feet;
Many a time for me have they
Brought the tall red deer to bay.

Oh! to hear my true Love singing,
Sweet as sound of trumpets ringing:
Like the sway of ocean swelling
Roll'd his deep voice round our dwelling.

Oh! to hear the echoes pealing
Round our green and fairy sheeling,
When the Three, with soaring chorus,
Pass'd the silent skylark o'er us.

Echo now, sleep, morn and even—
Lark alone enchant the heaven!—
Ardan's lips are scant of breath,—
Neesa's tongue is cold in death.

Stag, exult on glen and mountain—
Salmon, leap from loch to fountain—
Heron, in the free air warm ye—
Usnach's Sons no more will harm ye!

Erin's stay no more you are,
Rulers of the ridge of war;
Never more 'twill be your fate
To keep the beam of battle straight.

Woe is me! by fraud and wrong—
Traitors false and tyrants strong—
Fell Clan Usnach, bought and sold,
For Barach's feast and Conor's gold!

Woe to Eman, roof and wall!—
Woe to Red Branch, hearth and hall!—
Tenfold woe and black dishonour
To the false and foul Clan Conor!

Dig the grave both wide and deep,
Sick I am, and fain would sleep!
Dig the grave and make it ready,
Lay me on my true Love's body.

THE FAREWELL
ROBERT BURNS (1759 – 1796)

IRISCHE SOLDATEN (IRISH MERCENARIES)
by Albrecht Dürer. 1521. Engraving.
Kupferstichkabinett, Staatliche Museen Preussischer
Kulturbesitz, West Berlin

*Dürer saw these soldiers when they were employed
on the Continent.*

It was a' for our rightfu' King
  We left fair Scotland's strand;
It was a' for our rightfu' King
  We e'er saw Irish land,
      My dear—
  We e'er saw Irish land.

Now a' is done that men can do,
  And a' is done in vain;
My love and native land, farewell,
  For I maun cross the main,
      My dear—
  For I maun cross the main.

He turn'd him right and round about
  Upon the Irish shore;
And gae his bridle-reins a shake,
  With, Adieu for evermore,
      My dear—
  With, Adieu for evermore!

The sodger frae the wars returns,
  The sailor frae the main;
But I hae parted frae my love,
  Never to meet again,
      My dear—
  Never to meet again.

When day is gane, and night is come,
  And a' folk bound to sleep,
I think on him that's far awa',
  The lee-lang night, and weep,
      My dear—
  The lee-lang night, and weep.

THE MEMORY OF THE DEAD

JOHN KELLS INGRAM (1823–1907)

Who fears to speak of Ninety-Eight?
  Who blushes at the name?
When cowards mock the patriot's fate,
  Who hangs his head for shame?
He's all a knave or half a slave
  Who slights his country thus:
But a true man, like you, man,
  Will fill your glass with us.

We drink the memory of the brave,
  The faithful and the few—
Some lie far off beyond the wave,
  Some sleep in Ireland, too;
All, all are gone—but still lives on
  The fame of those who died;
And true men, like you, men,
  Remember them with pride.

Some on the shores of distant lands
  Their weary hearts have laid,
And by the stranger's heedless hands
  Their lonely graves were made;
But though their clay be far away
  Beyond the Atlantic foam,
In true men, like you, men,
  Their spirit's still at home.

The dust of some is Irish earth;
  Among their own they rest;
And the same land that gave them birth
  Has caught them to her breast;
And we will pray that from their clay
  Full many a race may start
Of true men, like you, men,
  To act as brave a part.

They rose in dark and evil days
  To right their native land;
They kindled here a living blaze
  That nothing shall withstand.
Alas! that Might can vanquish Right—
  They fell, and passed away;
But true men, like you, men,
  Are plenty here today.

Then here's their memory—may it be
  For us a guiding light,
To cheer our strife for liberty,
  And teach us to unite!
Through good and ill, be Ireland's still,
  Though sad as theirs, your fate;
And true men, be you, men,
  Like those of Ninety-Eight.

THE DUBLIN VOLUNTEERS IN COLLEGE GREEN, 4 NOVEMBER 1779
by Francis Wheatley. Late 18th century. Oil on canvas.
The National Gallery of Ireland, Dublin

AFTER DEATH

FANNY PARNELL (1854–1883)

THE AFFRAY AT THE WIDOW
MCCORMACK'S HOUSE,
ON BOULAGH COMMON.
Lithograph from ILLUSTRATED NEWS,
August 12, 1848.
National Library of Ireland, Dublin

Shall mine eyes behold thy glory, O my country? Shall mine eyes
     behold thy glory?
Or shall the darkness close around them, ere the sun-blaze break at
     last upon thy story?

When the nations ope for thee their queenly circle, as a sweet new
     sister hail thee,
Shall these lips be sealed in callous death and silence, that have known
     but to bewail thee?

Shall the ear be deaf that only loved thy praises, when all men their
     tribute bring thee?
Shall the mouth be clay that sang thee in thy squalor, when all poets'
     mouths shall sing thee?

Ah! the harpings and the salvos and the shoutings of thy exiled sons
     returning!
I should hear, tho' dead and mouldered, and the grave-damps should
     not chill my bosom's burning.

Ah! the tramp of feet victorious! I should hear them 'mid the
     shamrocks and the mosses,
And my heart should toss within the shroud and quiver as a captive
     dreamer tosses.

I should turn and rend the cere-clothes round me, giant sinews I
     should borrow—
Crying, "O, my brothers, I have also loved her in her loneliness and
     sorrow.

"Let me join with you the jubilant procession; let me chant with you
     her story;
Then contented I shall go back to the shamrocks, now mine eyes have
     seen her glory!"

JOHNNY, I HARDLY KNEW YE

STREET BALLAD (19TH CENTURY)

While going the road to sweet Athy,
    Hurroo! hurroo!
While going the road to sweet Athy,
    Hurroo! hurroo!
While going the road to sweet Athy,
A stick in my hand and a drop in my eye,
A doleful damsel I heard cry:—
"Och, Johnny, I hardly knew you.
With drums and guns and guns and drums,
    The enemy nearly slew ye,
    My darling dear, you look so queer,
Och, Johnny, I hardly knew ye!

"Where are your eyes that looked so mild?
    Hurroo! hurroo!
Where are your eyes that looked so mild?
    Hurroo! hurroo!
Where are your eyes that looked so mild,
When my poor heart you first beguiled?
Why did you run from me and the child?
    Och, Johnny, I hardly knew ye!
With drums, etc.

"Where are the legs with which you run?
    Hurroo! hurroo!
Where are the legs with which you run?
    Hurroo! hurroo!
Where are the legs with which you run,
When you went to carry a gun?—
Indeed, your dancing days are done!
    Och, Johnny, I hardly knew ye!
With drums, etc.

"It grieved my heart to see you sail,
    Hurroo! hurroo!
It grieved my heart to see you sail,
    Hurroo! hurroo!
It grieved my heart to see you sail,
Though from my heart you took leg bail,—
Like a cod you're doubled up head and tail.
    Och, Johnny, I hardly knew ye!
With drums, etc.

"You haven't an arm and you haven't a leg,
    Hurroo! hurroo!
You haven't an arm and you haven't a leg,
    Hurroo! hurroo!
You haven't an arm and you haven't a leg,
You're an eyeless, noseless, chickenless egg;
You'll have to be put in a bowl to beg:
    Och, Johnny, I hardly knew ye!
With drums, etc.

"I'm happy for to see you home,
    Hurroo! hurroo!
I'm happy for to see you home,
    Hurroo! hurroo!
I'm happy for to see you home,
All from the island of Sulloon,
So low in flesh, so high in bone,
    Och, Johnny, I hardly knew ye!
With drums, etc.

"But sad as it is to see you so,
    Hurroo! hurroo!
But sad as it is to see you so,
    Hurroo! hurroo!
But sad as it is to see you so,
And to think of you now as an object of woe,
Your Peggy'll still keep ye on as her beau;
    Och, Johnny, I hardly knew ye!

"With drums and guns and guns and drums,
    The enemy nearly slew ye,
    My darling dear, you look so queer,
Och, Johnny, I hardly knew ye!"

MILITARY MANEUVERS by Richard T. Moynan.
1891. Oil on canvas.
The National Gallery of Ireland, Dublin

MICHAEL COLLINS — FOR THE LOVE OF IRELAND
by Sir John Lavery. 1922. Oil on canvas.
Presented by the Artist, 1935, to The Hugh Lane
Municipal Gallery of Modern Art, Dublin

POEM

CHARLES DONNELLY (1914 – 1937)

Between rebellion as a private study and the public
Defiance is simple action only which will flicker
Catlike, for spring. Whether at nerve-roots is secret
Iron, there's no diviner can tell, only the moment can show.
Simple and unclear moment, on a morning utterly different
And under circumstances different from what you'd expected.

Your flag is public over granite. Gulls fly above it.
Whatever the issue of the battle is, your memory
Is public, for them to pull awry with crooked hands,
Moist eyes. And villages' reputations will be built on
Inaccurate accounts of your campaigns. You're name for orators,
Figure stone-struck beneath damp Dublin sky.

In a delaying action, perhaps, on hillside in remote parish,
Outposts correctly placed, retreat secured to wood, bridge mined
Against pursuit, sniper may sight you carelessly contoured.
Or death may follow years in strait confinement, where diet
Is uniform as ceremony, lacking only fruit
Or on the barracks square before the sun casts shadow.

Name, subject of all considered words, praise and blame
Irrelevant, the public talk which sounds the same on hollow
Tongue as true, you'll be with Parnell and with Pearse.
Name alderman will raise a cheer with, teacher make reference
Oblique in class, and boys and women spin gum of sentiment
On qualities attributed in error.

Man, dweller in mountain huts, possessor of colored mice,
Skilful in minor manual turns, patron of obscure subjects, of
Gaelic swordsmanship and medieval armory,
The technique of the public man, the masked servilities are
Not for you, Master of military trade, you give
Like Raleigh, Lawrence, Childers, your services but not yourself.

REVOLUTIONARY REVOLUTION
GEORGE BUCHANAN (BORN 1904)

Insidious in ways no gunfire touches, revolution
must have revolution in it too,
not be the same old murder.

The cry for a tender
style has never been so truly from the heart,
so treated as nothing much.

ENEMY ENCOUNTER
PADRAIC FIACC (BORN 1924)
(PATRICK JOSEPH O'CONNOR)
FOR LILAC

Dumping (left over from the autumn)
Dead leaves, near a culvert
I come on
            a British Army Soldier
With a rifle and a radio
Perched hiding. He has red hair.

He is young enough to be my weenie
-bopper daughter's boy-friend.
He is like a lonely little winter robin.

We are that close to each other, I
Can nearly hear his heart beating.

I say something bland to make him grin,
But his glass eyes look past my side
-whiskers down
            the Shore Road street.
I am an Irish man
            and he is afraid
That I have come to kill him.

British patrol on the border, Northern Ireland.
Photograph by Jill Uris

THE FAMINE YEAR

LADY JANE WILDE (1820–1896)

Weary men, what reap ye?—"Golden corn for the stranger."
What sow ye?—"Human corses that await for the Avenger."
Fainting forms, all hunger-stricken, what see you in the offing?
"Stately ships to bear our food away amid the stranger's scoffing."
There's a proud array of soldiers—what do they round your door?
"They guard our master's granaries from the thin hands of the poor."
Pale mothers, wherefore weeping?—"Would to God that we were dead—
Our children swoon before us, and we cannot give them bread!"

Little children, tears are strange upon your infant faces,
God meant you but to smile within your mother's soft embraces.
"Oh! we know not what is smiling, and we know not what is dying;
But we're hungry, very hungry, and we cannot stop our crying;
And some of us grow cold and white—we know not what it means.
But as they lie beside us we tremble in our dreams."
There's a gaunt crowd on the highway—are ye come to pray to man,
With hollow eyes that cannot weep, and for words your faces wan?

"No; the blood is dead within our veins; we care not now for life;
Let us die hid in the ditches, far from children and from wife;
We cannot stay to listen to their raving, famished cries—
Bread! Bread! Bread!—and none to still their agonies.
We left an infant playing with her dead mother's hand:
We left a maiden maddened by the fever's scorching brand:
Better, maiden, thou wert strangled in thy own dark-twisted tresses!
Better, infant, thou wert smothered in thy mother's first caresses.

DEATH WAGONS IN COUNTY CORK, 1847. Lithograph. National Library of Ireland, Dublin

"We are fainting in our misery, but God will hear our groan;
Yea, if fellow-men desert us, He will hearken from His throne!
Accursed are we in our own land, yet toil we still and toil;
But the stranger reaps our harvest—the alien owns our soil.
O Christ, how have we sinned, that on our native plains
We perish houseless, naked, starved, with branded brow, like Cain's?
Dying, dying wearily, with a torture sure and slow—
Dying as a dog would die, by the wayside as we go.

"One by one they're falling round us, their pale faces to the sky;
We've no strength left to dig them graves—there let them lie.
The wild bird, when he's stricken, is mourned by the others,
But we, we die in Christian land—we die amid our brothers—
In the land which God has given—like a wild beast in his cave,
Without a tear, a prayer, a shroud, a coffin, or a grave.
Ha! but think ye the contortions on each dead face ye see,
Shall not be read on judgement-day by the eyes of Deity?

"We are wretches, famished, scorned, human tools to build your pride,
But God will yet take vengeance for the souls for whom Christ died.
Now is your hour of pleasure, bask ye in the world's caress;
But our whitening bones against ye will arise as witnesses,
From the cabins and the ditches, in their charred, uncoffined masses,
For the ANGEL OF THE TRUMPET will know them as he passes.
A ghastly, spectral army before great God we'll stand
And arraign ye as our murderers, O spoilers of our land!"

IRISH PEASANTS LOOT A GALWAY POTATO STORE DURING THE GREAT FAMINE.
Lithograph. c. 1845–50. The New York Public Library Picture Collection

THE HUNGRY GRASS

DONAGH MACDONAGH (1912–1968)

Crossing the shallow holdings high above sea
Where few birds nest, the luckless foot may pass
From the bright safety of experience
Into the terror of the hungry grass.

Here in a year when poison from the air
First withered in despair the growth of spring
Some skull-faced wretch whom nettle could not save
Crept on four bones to his last scattering,

Crept, and the shrivelled heart which drove his thought
Towards platters brought in hospitality
Burst as the wizened eyes measured the miles
Like dizzy walls forbidding him the city.

Little the earth reclaimed from that poor body,
And yet remembering him the place has grown
Bewitched and the thin grass he nourishes
Racks with his famine, sucks marrow from the bone.

THE RETURNED PICTURE

MARY O'DONOVAN ROSSA (1845 – C. 1900)

Refused admission! Baby, Baby,
   Don't you feel a little pain?
See, your picture with your mother's,
   From the prison back again.
They are cruel, cruel jailors,—
   They are heartless, heartless men.

Ah, you laugh, my little Flax-Hair!
   But my eyes are full of tears;
And my heart is sorely troubled
   With old voices in my ears:
With the lingering disappointment
   That is shadowing my years!

Was it much to ask them, Baby—
   These rough menials of the Queen—
Was it much to ask, to give him
   This poor picture, form and mien
Of the wife he loved, the little son
   He never yet had seen?

Ah, they're cruel, cruel jailors;
   They are heartless, heartless men:
To bar the last poor comfort from
   Your father's prison pen;
To shut our picture from the gates
   And send it home again!

REMEMBERING CON MARKIEVICZ

C. DAY LEWIS (1904–1972)

Child running wild in woods of Lissadell:
Young lady from the Big House, seen
In a flowered dress gathering wild flowers: Ascendancy queen
Of hunts, house-parties, practical jokes—who could foretell
(*Oh fiery shade, impetuous bone*)
Where all was regular, self-sufficient, gay,
Their lovely hoyden lost in a nation's heroine?
Laughterless now the sweet demesne,
And the gaunt house looks blank on Sligo Bay
A nest decayed, an eagle flown.

The Paris studio, your playboy Count
Were not enough, nor Castle splendour
And fame of horsemanship. You were the tinder
Waiting a match, a runner tuned for the pistol's sound,
Impatient shade, long-suffering bone.
In a Balally cottage you found a store
Of Sinn Fein papers. You read (maybe the old sheets can while
The time). The flash lights up a whole
Ireland which you have never known before,
A nest betrayed, its eagles gone.

The road to Connolly and Stephen's Green
Showed clear. The great heart which defied
Irish prejudice, English snipers, died
A little not to have shared a grave with the fourteen.
Oh fiery shade, intransigent bone!
And when the Treaty emptied the British jails,
A haggard woman returned and Dublin went wild to greet her
But still it was not enough: an iota
Of compromise, she cried, and the Cause fails
Nest disarrayed, eagles undone.

Fanatic, bad actress, figure of fun—
She was called each. Ever she dreamed,
Fought, suffered for a losing side, it seems,
(The side which always at last is seen to have won).
Oh fiery shade and unvexed bone!
Remember a heart impulsive, gay and tender,
Still to an ideal Ireland and its real poor alive.
When she died in a pauper bed, in love
All the poor of Dublin rose to lament her.
A nest is made, an eagle flown.

CONSTANCE, COUNTESS MARKIEVICZ
by Casimir de Markievicz.
Early 20th century. Oil on canvas.
The National Gallery of Ireland, Dublin

Portrait of the Irish heroine
(née Constance Gore-Booth) by her husband.

ON A POLITICAL PRISONER

W. B. YEATS (1865 – 1939)

She that but little patience knew,
From childhood on, had now so much
A grey gull lost its fear and flew
Down to her cell and there alit,
And there endured her fingers' touch
And from her fingers ate its bit.

Did she in touching that lone wing
Recall the years before her mind
Became a bitter, an abstract thing,
Her thought some popular enmity:
Blind and leader of the blind
Drinking the foul ditch where they lie?

When long ago I saw her ride
Under Ben Bulben to the meet,
The beauty of her country-side
With all youth's lonely wildness stirred,
She seemed to have grown clean and sweet
Like any rock-bred, sea-borne bird:

Sea-borne, or balanced on the air
When first it sprang out of the nest
Upon some lofty rock to stare
Upon the cloudy canopy,
While under its storm-beaten breast
Cried out the hollows of the sea.

THE BOYNE WATER

ANONYMOUS (19TH CENTURY)

July the first, of a morning clear, one thousand six hundred and ninety,
King William did his men prepare—of thousands he had thirty—
To fight King James and all his foes, encamped near the Boyne Water;
He little feared, though two to one, their multitude to scatter.

King William called his officers, saying: "Gentlemen, mind your station,
And let your valour here be shown before this Irish nation;
My brazen walls let no man break, and your subtle foes you'll scatter,
Be sure you show them good English play as you go over the water."

Both foot and horse they marched on, intending them to batter,
But the brave Duke Schomberg he was shot as he crossed over the water.
When that King William did observe the brave Duke Schomberg falling,
He reined his horse with a heavy heart, on the Enniskillenes calling:

"What will you do for me, brave boys—see yonder men retreating?
Our enemies encouraged are, and English drums are beating."
He says, "My boys feel no dismay at the losing of one commander,
For God shall be our King this day, and I'll be general under."

Within four yards of our fore-front, before a shot was fired,
A sudden snuff they got that day, which little they desired;
For horse and man fell to the ground, and some hung on their saddle:
Others turned up their forked ends, which we call coup de ladle.

Prince Eugene's regiment was the next, on our right hand advanced
Into a field of standing wheat, where Irish horses pranced;
But the brandy ran so in their heads, their senses all did scatter,
They little thought to leave their bones that day at the Boyne Water.

THE BATTLE OF THE BOYNE, 1690 by Jan Wyck.
1693. Oil on canvas.
The National Gallery of Ireland, Dublin.
Bequest of G. Jameson, 1936

Both men and horse lay on the ground, and many there lay bleeding,
I saw no sickles there that day—but, sure, there was sharp shearing.
Now, praise God, all true Protestants, and heaven's and earth's Creator,
For the deliverance he sent our enemies to scatter.

The Church's foes will pine away, like churlish-hearted Nabal,
For our deliverer came this day like the great Zorobabal.
So praise God, all true Protestants, and I will say no further,
But had the Papists gained that day, there would have been open murder.
Although King James and many more were ne'er that way inclined,
It was not in their power to stop what the rabble they designed.

TWELFTH OF JULY, PORTADOWN, 1928
by Sir John Lavery. c. 1928.
Oil on canvas. Ulster Museum, Belfast.
Donated by the artist

A traditional parade of the
Orangemen in Northern Ireland.

ULSTER (1912)

RUDYARD KIPLING (1865 – 1936)

(*"Their webs shall not become garments, neither shall*
they cover themselves with their works: their works
are works of iniquity and the act of violence is in their
hands."—ISAIAH lix. 6.)

The dark eleventh hour
Draws on and sees us sold
To every evil power
We fought against of old.
Rebellion, rapine, hate,
Oppression, wrong and greed
Are loosed to rule our fate
By England's act and deed.

The Faith in which we stand,
The laws we made and guard—
Our honour, lives, and land—
Are given for reward
To Murder done by night,
To Treason taught by day,
To folly, sloth, and spite,
And we are thrust away.

The blood our fathers spilt,
Our love, our toils, our pains,
Are counted us for guilt,
And only bind our chains.
Before an Empire's eyes
The traitor claims his price.
What need of further lies?
We are the sacrifice.

We asked no more than leave
To reap where we had sown,
Through good and ill to cleave
To our own flag and throne.
Now England's shot and steel
Beneath that flag must show
How loyal hearts should kneel
To England's oldest foe.

We know the wars prepared
On every peaceful home,
We know the hells declared
For such as serve not Rome—
The terror, threats, and dread
In market, hearth, and field—
We know, when all is said,
We perish if we yield.

Believe, we dare not boast,
Believe, we do not fear—
We stand to pay the cost
In all that men hold dear.
What answer from the North?
One Law, one Land, one Throne.
If England drive us forth
We shall not fall alone!

THE GARDENER
FROM NOVELETTES III

LOUIS MACNEICE (1907–1963)

He was not able to read or write,
He did odd jobs on gentlemen's places
Cutting the hedge or hoeing the drive
With the smile of a saint,
With the pride of a feudal chief,
For he was not quite all there.

Crippled by rheumatism
By the time his hair was white,
He would reach the garden by twelve
His legs in soiled puttees,
A clay pipe in his teeth,
A tiny flag in his cap,
A white cat behind him,
And his eyes a cornflower blue.

And between the clack of the shears
Or the honing of the scythe
Or the rattle of the rake on the gravel
He would talk to amuse the children,
He would talk to himself or the cat
Or the robin waiting for worms
Perched on the handle of the spade;
Would remember snatches of verse
From the elementary school
About a bee and a wasp
Or the cat by the barndoor spinning;
And would talk about himself for ever—
You would never find his like—
Always in the third person;
And would level his stick like a gun
(With a glint in his eye)
Saying "Now I'm a Frenchman"—
He was not quite right in the head.

He believed in God—
The Good Fellow Up There—
And he used a simile of Homer
Watching the falling leaves,
And every year he waited for the Twelfth of July,
Cherishing his sash and his fife
For the carnival of banners and drums.
He was always claiming but never
Obtaining his old age pension,
For he did not know his age.

And his rheumatism at last
Kept him out of the processions.
And he came to work in the garden
Later and later in the day,
Leaving later at night;
In the damp dark of the night
At ten o'clock or later
You could hear him mowing the lawn,
The mower moving forward,
And backward, forward and backward
For he mowed while standing still;
He was not quite up to the job.

But he took a pride in the job,
He kept a bowl of cold
Tea in the crotch of a tree,
Always enjoyed his food
And enjoyed honing the scythe
And making the potato drills
And putting the peasticks in;
And enjoyed the noise of the corncrake,
And the early hawthorn hedge
Peppered black and green,
And the cut grass dancing in the air—
Happy as the day was long.

Till his last sickness took him
And he could not leave his house
And his eyes lost their colour
And he sat by the little range
With a finch in a cage and a framed
Certificate of admission
Into the Orange Order,
And his speech began to wander
And memory ebbed
Leaving upon the shore
Odd shells and heads of wrack
And his soul went out on the ebbing
Tide in a trim boat
To find the Walls of Derry
Or the land of the Ever Young.

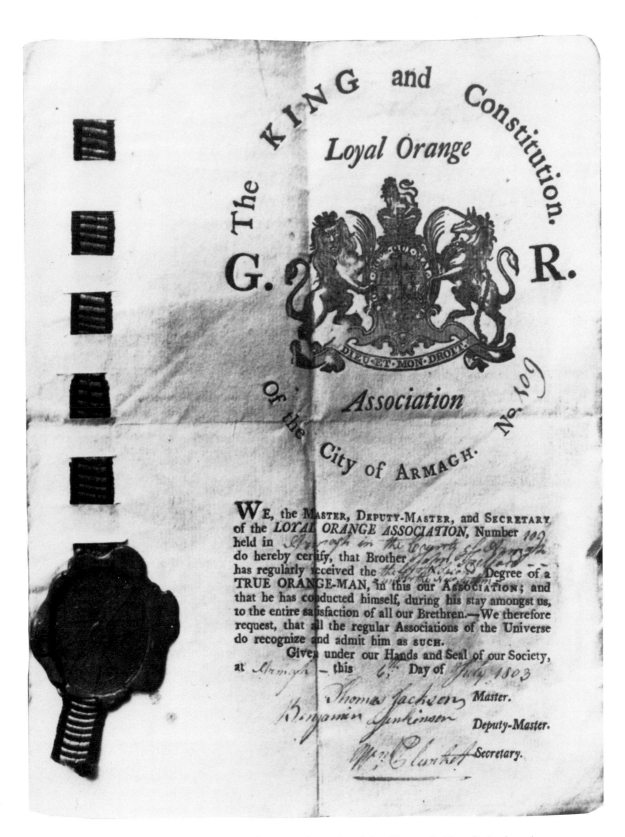

The KING and Constitution.

Loyal Orange

G. R.

DIEU · ET · MON · DROIT.

Association

of the City of ARMAGH.

No. 109

WE, the MASTER, DEPUTY-MASTER, and SECRETARY of the *LOYAL ORANGE ASSOCIATION*, Number 109 held in *Armagh in the County of Armagh* do hereby certify, that Brother *John Telford* has regularly received the *........* Degree of a TRUE ORANGE-MAN, in this our ASSOCIATION; and that he has conducted himself, during his stay amongst us, to the entire satisfaction of all our Brethren.—We therefore request, that all the regular Associations of the Universe do recognize and admit him as SUCH.

Given under our Hands and Seal of our Society, at *Armagh* — this *6th* Day of *July 1803*

Thomas Jackson Master.

Benjamin Jenkinson Deputy-Master.

Wm. Blanket Secretary.

Early membership certificate for the Armagh branch of the Loyal Orange Association. Photograph. Alison Studio, Armagh

Women unloading guns on the AASGARD, a ship that smuggled arms into Howth for the Irish volunteers in July 1914. Photograph. National Library of Ireland, Dublin

THE WEARING OF THE GREEN

STREET BALLAD (1798)

O Paddy dear, and did you hear the news that's going round?
The shamrock is forbid by law to grow on Irish ground;
St. Patrick's day no more we'll keep, his colours can't be seen,
For there's a bloody law again the wearing of the green.
I met with Napper Tandy, and he took me by the hand,
And he said, "How's poor old Ireland, and how does she stand?"
She's the most distressful country that ever yet was seen,
They are hanging men and women for the wearing of the green.

Then since the colour we must wear is England's cruel red,
Sure Ireland's sons will ne'er forget the blood that they have shed.
You may take the shamrock from your hat and cast it on the sod,
But 'twill take root and flourish there, though under foot 'tis trod.
When law can stop the blades of grass from growing as they grow,
And when the leaves in summer-time their verdure dare not show,
Then I will change the colour that I wear in my caubeen,
But 'till that day, please God, I'll stick to wearing of the green.

But if at last our colour should be torn from Ireland's heart,
Her sons with shame and sorrow from the dear old isle will part;
I've heard a whisper of a country that lies beyond the sea,
Where rich and poor stand equal in the light of freedom's day.
O Erin, must we leave you, driven by a tyrant's hand?
Must we ask a mother's blessing from a strange and distant land?
Where the cruel cross of England shall nevermore be seen,
And where, please God, we'll live and die still wearing of the green.

EASTER 1916

W. B. YEATS (1865–1939)

I have met them at close of day
Coming with vivid faces
From counter or desk among grey
Eighteenth-century houses.
I have passed with a nod of the head
Or polite meaningless words,
Or have lingered awhile and said
Polite meaningless words,
And thought before I had done
Of a mocking tale or a gibe
To please a companion
Around the fire at the club,
Being certain that they and I
But lived where motley is worn:
All changed, changed utterly:
A terrible beauty is born.

That woman's days were spent
In ignorant good-will,
Her nights in argument
Until her voice grew shrill.
What voice more sweet than hers
When, young and beautiful,
She rode to harriers?
This man had kept a school
And rode our wingèd horse;
This other his helper and friend
Was coming into his force;
He might have won fame in the end,
So sensitive his nature seemed,
So daring and sweet his thought.
This other man I had dreamed
A drunken, vainglorious lout.
He had done most bitter wrong
To some who are near my heart,
Yet I number him in the song;
He, too, has resigned his part
In the casual comedy;
He, too, has been changed in his turn,
Transformed utterly:
A terrible beauty is born.

Hearts with one purpose alone
Through summer and winter seem
Enchanted to a stone
To trouble the living stream.
The horse that comes from the road,
The rider, the birds that range
From cloud to tumbling cloud,
Minute by minute they change;
A shadow of cloud on the stream
Changes minute by minute;
A horse-hoof slides on the brim,
And a horse plashes within it;
The long-legged moor-hens dive,
And hens to moor-cocks call;
Minute by minute they live:
The stone's in the midst of all.

Too long a sacrifice
Can make a stone of the heart.
O when may it suffice?
That is Heaven's part, our part
To murmur name upon name,
As a mother names her child
When sleep at last has come
On limbs that had run wild.
What is it but nightfall?
No, no, not night but death;
Was it needless death after all?
For England may keep faith
For all that is done and said.
We know their dream; enough
To know they dreamed and are dead;
And what if excess of love
Bewildered them till they died?
I write it out in a verse—
MacDonagh and MacBride
And Connolly and Pearse
Now and in time to be,
Wherever green is worn,
Are changed, changed utterly:
A terrible beauty is born.

September 25, 1916

Irish rebellion. Members of the British army policing the interior of the bombed-out General Post Office, May 1916.
Photograph. The Bettmann Archive, New York

View of the General Post Office, the rebel headquarters, several days after the 1916 Rising. Photograph. National Library of Ireland, Dublin

I AM IRELAND

PATRICK PEARSE (1879 – 1916)

I am Ireland:
I am older than the Old Woman of Beare.

Great my glory:
I that bore Cuchulainn the valiant.

Great my shame:
My own children that sold their mother.

I am Ireland:
I am lonelier than the Old Woman of Beare.

WILLIAM BUTLER YEATS, POET by John Butler Yeats. 1900.
Oil on canvas. The National Gallery of Ireland, Dublin

One of several portraits of the poet by his father.

BROWN PENNY

W. B. YEATS (1865 – 1939)

I whispered, "I am too young,"
And then, "I am old enough";
Wherefore I threw a penny
To find out if I might love.
"Go and love, go and love, young man,
If the lady be young and fair."
Ah, penny, brown penny, brown penny,
I am looped in the loops of her hair.

O love is the crooked thing,
There is nobody wise enough
To find out all that is in it,
For he would be thinking of love
Till the stars had run away
And the shadows eaten the moon.
Ah, penny, brown penny, brown penny,
One cannot begin it too soon.

TO A CHILD DANCING IN THE WIND

W. B. YEATS (1865 – 1939)

Dance there upon the shore;
What need have you to care
For wind or water's roar?
And tumble out your hair
That the salt drops have wet;
Being young you have not known
The fool's triumph, nor yet
Love lost as soon as won,
Nor the best labourer dead
And all the sheaves to bind.
What need have you to dread
The monstrous crying of wind?

William Butler Yeats at Lennox Robinson's cottage. c. 1933.
Photograph by S. J. McCormack. Robert W. Woodruff Library, Special Collections, Emory University, Atlanta

FRIENDS

W. B. YEATS (1865 – 1939)

Now must I these three praise—
Three women that have wrought
What joy is in my days:
One because no thought,
Nor those unpassing cares,
No, not in these fifteen
Many-times-troubled years,
Could ever come between
Mind and delighted mind;
And one because her hand
Had strength that could unbind
What none can understand,
What none can have and thrive,
Youth's dreamy load, till she
So changed me that I live
Labouring in ecstasy.

And what of her that took
All till my youth was gone
With scarce a pitying look?
How could I praise that one?
When day begins to break
I count my good and bad,
Being wakeful for her sake,
Remembering what she had,
What eagle look still shows,
While up from my heart's root
So great a sweetness flows
I shake from head to foot.

AUGUSTA GREGORY, DRAMATIST by John Butler Yeats.
1903. Oil on canvas. The National Gallery of Ireland, Dublin

Lady Gregory played a vital part in the rebirth of Irish theater.

COOLE PARK, 1929

W . B . Y E A T S (1865–1939)

I meditate upon a swallow's flight,
Upon an aged woman and her house,
A sycamore and lime-tree lost in night
Although that western cloud is luminous,
Great works constructed there in nature's spite
For scholars and for poets after us,
Thoughts long knitted into a single thought,
A dance-like glory that those walls begot.

There Hyde before he had beaten into prose
That noble blade the Muses buckled on,
There one that ruffled in a manly pose
For all his timid heart, there that slow man,
That meditative man, John Synge, and those
Impetuous men, Shawe-Taylor and Hugh Lane
Found pride established in humility,
A scene well set and excellent company.

They came like swallows and like swallows went,
And yet a woman's powerful character
Could keep a swallow to its first intent;
And half a dozen in formation there,
That seemed to whirl upon a compass-point,
Found certainty upon the dreaming air,
The intellectual sweetness of those lines
That cut through time or cross it withershins.

Here, traveller, scholar, poet, take your stand
When all those rooms and passages are gone,
When nettles wave upon a shapeless mound
And saplings root among the broken stone,
And dedicate—eyes bent upon the ground,
Back turned upon the brightness of the sun
And all the sensuality of the shade—
A moment's memory to that laurelled head.

A PRAYER FOR OLD AGE

W . B . Y E A T S (1865–1939)

God guard me from those thoughts men think
In the mind alone;
He that sings a lasting song
Thinks in a marrow-bone;

From all that makes a wise old man
That can be praised of all;
O what am I that I should not seem
For the song's sake a fool?

I pray—for fashion's word is out
And prayer comes round again—
That I may seem, though I die old,
A foolish, passionate man.

UNDER BEN BULBEN

W. B. YEATS (1865–1939)

William Butler Yeats's gravestone in Drumcliff, Co. Sligo.
Photograph: Irish Tourist Board, Dublin

I

Swear by what the sages spoke
Round the Mareotic Lake
That the Witch of Atlas knew,
Spoke and set the cocks a-crow.

Swear by those horsemen, by those women
Complexion and form prove superhuman,
That pale, long-visaged company
That air in immortality
Completeness of their passions won;
Now they ride the wintry dawn
Where Ben Bulben sets the scene.

Here's the gist of what they mean.

II

Many times man lives and dies
Between his two eternities,
That of race and that of soul,
And ancient Ireland knew it all.
Whether man die in his bed
Or the rifle knock him dead,
A brief parting from those dear
Is the worst man has to fear.
Though grave-diggers' toil is long,
Sharp their spades, their muscles strong,
They but thrust their buried men
Back in the human mind again.

III

You that Mitchel's prayer have heard,
"Send war in our time, O Lord!"
Know that when all words are said
And a man is fighting mad,
Something drops from eyes long blind,
He completes his partial mind,
For an instant stands at ease,
Laughs aloud, his heart at peace.
Even the wisest man grows tense
With some sort of violence
Before he can accomplish fate,
Know his work or choose his mate.

IV

Poet and sculptor, do the work,
Nor let the modish painter shirk
What his great forefathers did,
Bring the soul of man to God,
Make him fill the cradles right.

Measurement began our might:
Forms a stark Egyptian thought,
Forms that gentler Phidias wrought.
Michael Angelo left a proof
On the Sistine Chapel roof,
Where but half-awakened Adam
Can disturb globe-trotting Madam
Till her bowels are in heat,
Proof that there's a purpose set
Before the secret working mind:
Profane perfection of mankind.

Quattrocento put in paint
On backgrounds for a God or Saint
Gardens where a soul's at ease;
Where everything that meets the eye,
Flowers and grass and cloudless sky,
Resemble forms that are or seem
When sleepers wake and yet still dream,
And when it's vanished still declare,
With only bed and bedstead there,
That heavens had opened.
                    Gyres run on;
When that greater dream had gone
Calvert and Wilson, Blake and Claude,
Prepared a rest for the people of God,
Palmer's phrase, but after that
Confusion fell upon our thought.

V

Irish poets, learn your trade,
Sing whatever is well made,
Scorn the sort now growing up
All out of shape from toe to top,
Their unremembering hearts and heads
Base-born products of base beds.
Sing the peasantry, and then
Hard-riding country gentlemen,
The holiness of monks, and after
Porter-drinkers' randy laughter;
Sing the lords and ladies gay
That were beaten into the clay
Through seven heroic centuries;
Cast your mind on other days
That we in coming days may be
Still the indomitable Irishry.

VI

Under bare Ben Bulben's head
In Drumcliff churchyard Yeats is laid.
An ancestor was rector there
Long years ago, a church stands near,
By the road an ancient cross.
No marble, no conventional phrase;
On limestone quarried near the spot
By his command these words are cut:

Cast a cold eye
On life, on death.
Horseman, pass by!

September 4, 1938

IN MEMORY OF W. B. YEATS (D. JAN. 1939)

W. H. AUDEN (1907–1963)

1

He disappeared in the dead of winter:
The brooks were frozen, the airports almost deserted,
And snow disfigured the public statues;
The mercury sank in the mouth of the dying day.
O all the instruments agree
The day of his death was a dark cold day.

Far from his illness
The wolves ran on through the evergreen forests,
The peasant river was untempted by the fashionable quays;
By mourning tongues
The death of the poet was kept from his poems.

But for him it was his last afternoon as himself,
An afternoon of nurses and rumours;
The provinces of his body revolted,
The squares of his mind were empty,
Silence invaded the suburbs,
The current of his feeling failed: he became his admirers.

Now he is scattered among a hundred cities
And wholly given over to unfamiliar affections;
To find his happiness in another kind of wood
And be punished under a foreign code of conscience.
The words of a dead man
Are modified in the guts of the living.

But in the importance and noise of tomorrow
When the brokers are roaring like beasts on the floor of the Bourse,
And the poor have the sufferings to which they are fairly accustomed,
And each in the cell of himself is almost convinced of his freedom;
A few thousand will think of this day
As one thinks of a day when one did something slightly unusual.
O all the instruments agree
The day of his death was a dark cold day.

2

You were silly like us: your gift survived it all;
The parish of rich women, physical decay,
Yourself; mad Ireland hurt you into poetry.
Now Ireland has her madness and her weather still,
For poetry makes nothing happen: it survives
In the valley of its saying where executives
Would never want to tamper; it flows south
From ranches of isolation and the busy griefs,
Raw towns that we believe and die in; it survives,
A way of happening, a mouth.

3

Earth, receive an honoured guest;
William Yeats is laid to rest:
Let the Irish vessel lie
Emptied of its poetry.

Time that is intolerant
Of the brave and innocent,
And indifferent in a week
To a beautiful physique,

Worships language and forgives
Everyone by whom it lives;
Pardons cowardice, conceit,
Lays its honours at their feet.

Time that with this strange excuse
Pardoned Kipling and his views,
And will pardon Paul Claudel,
Pardons him for writing well.

In the nightmare of the dark
All the dogs of Europe bark,
And the living nations wait,
Each sequestered in its hate;

Intellectual disgrace
Stares from every human face,
And the seas of pity lie
Locked and frozen in each eye.

Follow, poet, follow right
To the bottom of the night,
With your unconstraining voice
Still persuade us to rejoice;

With the farming of a verse
Make a vineyard of the curse,
Sing of human unsuccess
In a rapture of distress;

In the deserts of the heart
Let the healing fountain start,
In the prison of his days
Teach the free man how to praise.

THE CURSE OF CROMWELL

W. B. YEATS (1865 – 1939)

You ask what I have found, and far and wide I go:
Nothing but Cromwell's house and Cromwell's murderous crew,
The lovers and the dancers are beaten into the clay,
And the tall men and the swordsmen and the horsemen, where are they?
And there is an old beggar wandering in his pride—
His fathers served their fathers before Christ was crucified.
> *O what of that, O what of that,*
> *What is there left to say?*

All neighbourly content and easy talk are gone,
But there's no good complaining, for money's rant is on.
He that's mounting up must on his neighbour mount,
And we and all the Muses are things of no account.
They have schooling of their own, but I pass their schooling by,
What can they know that we know that know the time to die?
> *O what of that, O what of that,*
> *What is there left to say?*

But there's another knowledge that my heart destroys,
As the fox in the old fable destroyed the Spartan boy's,
Because it proves that things both can and cannot be;
That the swordsmen and the ladies can still keep company,
Can pay the poet for a verse and hear the fiddle sound,
That I am still their servant though all are underground.
> *O what of that, O what of that,*
> *What is there left to say?*

I came on a great house in the middle of the night,
Its open lighted doorway and its windows all alight,
And all my friends were there and made me welcome too;
But I woke in an old ruin that the winds howled through;
And when I pay attention I must out and walk
Among the dogs and horses that understand my talk.
> *O what of that, O what of that,*
> *What is there left to say?*

TO THE LORD GENERAL CROMWELL
(ON THE PROPOSALS OF CERTAIN MINISTERS AT THE COMMITTEE
FOR PROPAGATION OF THE GOSPEL)
JOHN MILTON (1608 – 1674)

Cromwell, our chief of men, who through a cloud
   Not of war only, but detractions rude,
   Guided by faith and matchless Fortitude,
   To peace and truth thy glorious way hast plough'd,
And on the neck of crowned Fortune proud
   Hast rear'd God's Trophies, and his work pursu'd,
   While Darwen stream with blood of Scots imbru'd,
   And Dunbar field resounds thy praises loud,
And Worcester's laureate wreath; yet much remains
   To conquer still; peace hath her victories
   No less renown'd than war, new foes arise
Threat'ning to bind our souls with secular chains:
   Help us to save free Conscience from the paw
   Of hireling wolves whose Gospel is their maw.

(May, 1652)

AN HORATIAN ODE UPON CROMWELL'S RETURN FROM IRELAND

ANDREW MARVELL (1621 – 1678)

The forward youth that would appear
Must now forsake his Muses dear,
    Nor in the shadows sing
    His numbers languishing.

'Tis time to leave the books in dust,
And oil the unused armour's rust,
    Removing from the wall
    The corslet of the hall.

So restless Cromwell could not cease
In the inglorious arts of peace,
    But through adventurous war
    Urgèd his active star:

And like the three-fork'd lightning, first
Breaking the clouds where it was nurst,
    Did thorough his own side
    His fiery way divide:

For 'tis all one to courage high,
The emulous, or enemy;
    And with such, to enclose
    Is more than to oppose.

Then burning through the air he went
And palaces and temples rent;
    And Caesar's head at last
    Did through his laurels blast.

'Tis madness to resist or blame
The face of angry Heaven's flame;
    And if we would speak true,
    Much to the man is due,

Who, from his private gardens, where
He lived reservèd and austere
    (As if his highest plot
    To plant the bergamot),

Could by industrious valour climb
To ruin the great work of time,
    And cast the Kingdoms old
    Into another mould;

Though Justice against Fate complain,
And plead the ancient rights in vain—
    But those do hold or break
    As men are strong or weak—

Nature, that hateth emptiness,
Allows of penetration less,
    And therefore must make room
    Where greater spirits come.

What field of all the civil war
Where his were not the deepest scar?
    And Hampton shows what part
    He had of wiser art;

Where, twining subtle fears with hope,
He wove a net of such a scope
    That Charles himself might chase
    To Carisbrook's narrow case;

That thence the Royal actor borne
The tragic scaffold might adorn:
    While round the armèd bands
    Did clap their bloody hands.

He nothing common did or mean
Upon that memorable scene,
    But with his keener eye
    The axe's edge did try;

Nor call'd the Gods, with vulgar spite,
To vindicate his helpless right;
    But bow'd his comely head
    Down, as upon a bed.

This was that memorable hour
Which first assured the forcèd power:
    So when they did design
    The Capitol's first line,

A Bleeding Head, where they begun,
Did fright the architects to run;
    And yet in that the State
    Foresaw its happy fate!

And now the Irish are ashamed
To see themselves in one year tamed:
    So much one man can do
    That does both act and know.

They can affirm his praises best,
And have, though overcome, confest
    How good he is, how just
    And fit for highest trust;

Nor yet grown stiffer with command,
But still in the Republic's hand—
    How fit he is to sway
    That can so well obey!

He to the Commons' feet presents
A Kingdom for his first year's rents,
    And, what he may, forbears
    His fame, to make it theirs:

And has his sword and spoils ungirt
To lay them at the public's skirt.
    So when the falcon high
    Falls heavy from the sky,

She, having kill'd, no more does search
But on the next green bough to perch,
    Where, when he first does lure,
    The falconer has her sure.

What may not then our Isle presume
While victory his crest does plume?
    What may not others fear,
    If thus he crowns each year?

As Caesar he, ere long, to Gaul,
To Italy an Hannibal,
    And to all States not free
    Shall climacteric be.

The Pict no shelter now shall find
Within his particolour'd mind,
    But, from this valour, sad
    Shrink underneath the plaid,

Happy, if in the tufted brake
The English hunter him mistake,
    Nor lay his hounds in near
    The Caledonian deer.

But thou, the War's and Fortune's son,
March indefatigably on;
    And for the last effect,
    Still keep the sword erect:

Besides the force it has to fright
The spirits of the shady night,
    The same arts that did gain
    A power, must it maintain.

Dubliners.
Photograph. c. 1900.
Collection Charles Sullivan

LADIES AND GENTS, YOU ARE HERE ASSEMBLED
FROM GAS FROM A BURNER
(ON THE REFUSAL OF AN IRISH FIRM TO PUBLISH *DUBLINERS*)
JAMES JOYCE (1882–1941)

Ladies and gents, you are here assembled
To hear why earth and heaven trembled
Because of the black and sinister arts
Of an Irish writer in foreign parts.
He sent me a book ten years ago.
I read it a hundred times or so,
Backwards and forwards, down and up,
Through both ends of a telescope.
I printed it all to the very last word
But by the mercy of the Lord
The darkness of my mind was rent
And I saw the writer's foul intent.
But I owe a duty to Ireland:
I hold her honour in my hand,
This lovely land that always sent
Her writers and artists to banishment
And in a spirit of Irish fun
Betrayed her own leaders, one by one.

JAMES JOYCE by Augustus John.
1930. Pencil on paper.
Photograph: Archiv für Kunst
und Geschichte, West Berlin

James Joyce

Augustus John.

Paris

1930

HERBERT STREET REVISITED

JOHN MONTAGUE (BORN 1929)

FOR MADELEINE

I

A light is burning late
in this Georgian Dublin street:
someone is leading our old lives!

And our black cat scampers again
through the wet grass of the convent garden
upon his masculine errands.

The pubs shut: a released bull,
Behan shoulders up the street,
topples into our basement, roaring "John!"

A pony and donkey cropped flank
by flank under the trees opposite;
short neck up, long neck down,

as Nurse Mullen knelt by her bedside
to pray for her lost Mayo hills,
the bruised bodies of Easter Volunteers.

Animals, neighbours, treading the pattern
of one time and place into history,
like our early marriage, while

tall windows looked down upon us
from walls flushed light pink or salmon
watching and enduring succession.

II

As I leave, you whisper,
"don't betray our truth"
and like a ghost dancer,
invoking a lost tribal strength
I halt in tree-fed darkness
to summon back our past,
and celebrate a love that eased
so kindly, the dying bone,
enabling the spirit to sing
of old happiness, when alone.

III

So put the leaves back on the tree,
put the tree back in the ground,
let Brendan trundle his corpse down
the street singing, like Molly Malone.

Let the black cat, tiny emissary
of our happiness, streak again
through the darkness, to fall soft
clawed into a landlord's dustbin.

Let Nurse Mullen take the last
train to Westport, and die upright
in her chair, facing a window
warm with the blue slopes of Nephin.

And let the pony and donkey come—
look, someone has left the gate open—
like hobbyhorses linked in
the slow motion of a dream

parading side by side, down
the length of Herbert Street,
rising and falling, lifting
their hooves through the moonlight.

CATS IN THE KITCHEN by Nano Reid.
c. 1953. Oil on panel.
The Hugh Lane Municipal Gallery
of Modern Art, Dublin

ESTHER JOHNSON (SWIFT'S "STELLA")
by James Latham. Early 18th century. Oil on canvas.
The National Gallery of Ireland, Dublin

ON STELLA'S BIRTHDAY, 1719

JONATHAN SWIFT (1667–1745)

Stella this day is thirty-four,
(We shan't dispute a year or more)
However Stella, be not troubled,
Although thy size and years are doubled,
Since first I saw thee at sixteen
The brightest virgin on the green,
So little is thy form declined
Made up so largely in thy mind.
Oh, would it please the gods to split
Thy beauty, size, and years, and wit,
No age could furnish out a pair
Of nymphs so graceful, wise and fair
With half the luster of your eyes,
With half your wit, your years and size:
And then before it grew too late,
How should I beg of gentle Fate,
(That either nymph might have her swain,)
To split my worship too in twain.

INSCRIPTION FOR A HEADSTONE

AUSTIN CLARKE (1896–1974)

What Larkin bawled to hungry crowds
Is murmured now in dining-hall
And study. Faith bestirs itself
Lest infidels in their impatience
Leave it behind. Who could have guessed
Batons were blessings in disguise,
When every ambulance was filled
With half-killed men and Sunday trampled
Upon unrest? Such fear can harden
Or soften heart, knowing too clearly
His name endures on our holiest page,
Scrawled in a rage by Dublin's poor.

James Larkin (1876–1947), Irish socialist and founder of the ITGWU.
Photograph. National Library of Ireland, Dublin

A COAT

W. B. YEATS (1865–1939)

I made my song a coat
Covered with embroideries
Out of old mythologies
From heel to throat;
But the fools caught it,
Wore it in the world's eyes
As though they'd wrought it.
Song, let them take it,
For there's more enterprise
In walking naked.

EOIN O'MAHONY ("THE POPE") by David Hone. 1966. Oil on canvas.
The National Gallery of Ireland, Dublin

133

TWO LOVERS IN A LANDSCAPE by Thomas Bridgeford.
Early 19th century. Oil on canvas.
The National Gallery of Ireland, Dublin

AN IRISH LOVE SONG

JOHN TODHUNTER (1839 – 1916)

O, you plant the pain in my heart with your wistful eyes,
    Girl of my choice, Maureen!
Will you drive me mad for the kisses your shy sweet mouth denies,
    Maureen!

Like a walking ghost I am, and no words to woo,
    White rose of the West, Maureen;
For it's pale you are, and the fear that's on you is over me too,
    Maureen!

Sure it's our complaint that's on us, asthore, this day,
    Bride of my dreams, Maureen;
The smart of the bee that stung us, his honey must cure, they say,
    Maureen!

I'll coax the light to your eyes, and the rose to your face,
    Mavourneen, my own Maureen,
When I feel the warmth of your breast, and your nest is my arms' embrace,
    Maureen!

O where was the King o' the World that day—only me,
    My one true love, Maureen,
And you the Queen with me there, and your throne in my heart, machree,
    Maureen!

PAIRED LIVES

W. R. RODGERS (1909 – 1969)

Though to strangers' approach
(Like swing doors cheek to cheek)
Presenting one smooth front
Of summed resistance and
Aligned resentment, yet,
On nearer view note how,
At the deflecting touch
Of intervening hand,
Each in its lonely arc
Reaches and rocks inward
(Retires and returns
Immediately to join
The other moiety).
Each singly yields to thrust,
Is hung on its own hinge
Of fear and hope, and in
Its own reticence rests.

JANUS MASK HEAD by Pat Connor.
1979. Ceramic.
Collection of An Chomhairle Ealaíon/The Arts Council, Ireland

RENEWAL BY HER ELEMENT

DENIS DEVLIN (1908 – 1959)

The hawthorn morning moving
Above the battlements,
Breast from breast of lover
Tears, reminds of difference
And body's raggedness.

Immune from resolution
Into common clay
Because I have not known you;
Self-content as birdsong
Scornful at night-breakage
You seem to me. I am
Fresh from a long absence.

O suave through surf lifting
My smile upon your mouth;
Limbs according to rhythm
Separating, closing;
Scarcely using my name,
Traveller through troubling gestures,
Only for rare embraces
Of prepared texture.
Your lips amused harden
My arms round you defiant,
You shirk my enwreathing
Language, and you smile,
Turning aside my hand
Through your breath's light leafage,

Preferring yourself reflected
In my body to me,
Preferring my image of you
To you whom I achieved.
Noise is curbed attentive,
The sea hangs on your lips:
What would I do less?

It is over now but once
Our fees were nothing more,
Each for use of the other
In mortgage, than a glance.
I knew the secret movements
Of the blood under your throat
And when we lay love-proven
Whispering legends to sleep
Braceleted in embrace
Your hands pouring on me
Fresh water of their caresses,
Breasts, nests of my tenderness,
All night was laced with praise.

Now my image faded
In the lucid fields
Of your eyes. Never again
Surprise for years, years.

My landscape is grey rain
Aslant on bent seas.

LOOKING OUT TO SEA by William Orpen.
1908–12. Oil on canvas.
The National Gallery of Ireland, Dublin

140

I WOULD LIKE MY LOVE TO DIE

SAMUEL BECKETT (1906–1989)

I would like my love to die
and the rain to be falling on the graveyard
and on me walking the streets
mourning her who thought she loved me

SAMUEL BECKETT, from
SIX STUDIES TOWARD AN IMAGE OF SAMUEL BECKETT
by Louis le Brocquy. 1979–80. Oil on canvas.
Private collection

I SHALL NOT DIE FOR THEE

DOUGLAS HYDE (1860–1949)

For thee I shall not die,
   Woman high of fame and name;
Foolish men thou mayest slay
   I and they are not the same.

Why should I expire
   For the fire of any eye,
Slender waist or swan-like limb,
   Is't for them that I should die?

The round breasts, the fresh skin,
   Cheeks crimson, hair so long and rich;
Indeed, indeed, I shall not die,
   Please God, not I, for any such.

The golden hair, the forehead thin,
   The chaste mien, the gracious ease,
The rounded heel, the languid tone,
   Fools alone find death from these.

Thy sharp wit, thy perfect calm,
   Thy thin palm like foam o' the sea;
Thy white neck, thy blue eye,
   I shall not die for thee.

Woman, graceful as the swan,
   A wise man did nurture me,
Little palm, white neck, bright eye;
   I shall not die for ye.

THE CAPTIVE by Wilfred de Glehn. c. 1935. Oil on canvas.
Crawford Municipal Art Gallery, Cork

WOMAN, DON'T BE TROUBLESOME

AUGUSTUS YOUNG (BORN 1943)
(JAMES HOGAN)

Woman, don't be troublesome,
though your husband I may be;
our two minds were once at one,
why withdraw your hand from me.

Put your mouth of strawberry
on my mouth, cream is your cheek;
wind round white arms about me,
and do not go back to sleep.

Stay with me my flighty maid,
and be done with betrayal;
tonight this bed is wellmade,
let us toss it without fail.

Shut your eyes to other men,
no more women will I see:
the milkwhite tooth of passion
is between us—or should be.

FIGURE RECLINING by Brian Ballard. 1983. Oil on canvas. Private collection

COMPANY

MICHAEL LONGLEY (BORN 1939)

I imagine a day when the children
Are drawers full of soft toys, photographs
Beside the only surviving copies
Of the books that summarise my lifetime,
And I have begun to look forward to
Retirement, second childhood, except that
Love has diminished to one high room
Below which the vigilantes patrol
While I attempt to make myself heard
Above the cacophonous plumbing, and you
Who are my solitary interpreter
Can bear my company for long enough
To lipread such fictions as I believe
Will placate remote customs officials,
The border guards, or even reassure
Anxious butchers, greengrocers, tradesmen
On whom we depend for our daily bread,
The dissemination of manuscripts,
News from the outside world, simple acts
Of such unpatriotic generosity
That until death we hesitate together
On the verge of an almost total silence:

Or else we are living in the country
In a far-off townland divided by
The distances it takes to overhear
A quarrel or the sounds of love-making,
Where even impoverished households
Can afford to focus binoculars
On our tiny windows, the curtains
That wear my motionless silhouette
As I sit late beside a tilley-lamp
And try to put their district on the map
And to name the fields for them, for you
Who busy yourself about the cottage,
Its thatch letting in, the tall grasses
And the rain leaning against the half-door,
Dust on the rafters and our collection
Of curious utensils, pots and pans
The only escape from which is the twice
Daily embarrassed journey to and from
The well we have choked with alder branches
For the cattle's safety, their hoofprints
A thirsty circle in the puddles,
Watermarks under all that we say.

Windowsill, Co. Waterford.
Photograph by Richard Fitzgerald

THE SINGER'S HOUSE
SEAMUS HEANEY (BORN 1939)

When they said Carrickfergus I could hear
the frosty echo of saltminers' picks.
I imagined it, chambered and glinting,
a township built of light.

What do we say any more
to conjure the salt of our earth?
So much comes and is gone
that should be crystal and kept

and amicable weathers
that bring up the grain of things,
their tang of season and store,
are all the packing we'll get.

So I say to myself *Gweebarra*
and its music hits off the place
like water hitting off granite.
I see the glittering sound

framed in your window,
knives and forks set on oilcloth,
and the seals' heads,
suddenly outlined, dark and intelligent.

People here used to believe
that drowned souls lived in the seals.
At spring tides they might change shape.
They loved music and swam in for a singer

who stood at the end of summer
in the mouth of a whitewashed turf-shed,
his shoulder to the jamb, his song
a rowboat far out in evening.

When you came here first you were always singing,
a hint of the clip of the pick
in your winnowing climb and attack.
Raise it again, man. We still believe what we hear.

SONG

EAVAN BOLAND (BORN 1945)

Where in blind files
Bats outsleep the frost
Water slips through stones
Too fast, too fast
For ice; afraid he'd slip
By me I asked him first.

Round as a bracelet
Clasping the wet grass,
An adder drowsed by berries
Which change blood to cess;
Dreading delay's venom
I risked the first kiss.

My skirt in my hand,
Lifting the hem high
I forded the river there;
Drops splashed my thigh.
Ahead of me at last
He turned at my cry:

"Look how the water comes
Boldly to my side;
See the waves attempt
What you have never tried."
He late that night
Followed the leaping tide.

The swans of Cong, Co. Galway. Photograph by Jill Uris

SWANS MATING

MICHAEL LONGLEY (BORN 1939)

Even now I wish that you had been there
Sitting beside me on the riverbank:
The cob and his pen sailing in rhythm
Until their small heads met and the final
Heraldic moment dissolved in ripples.

LIKE DOLMENS ROUND MY CHILDHOOD, THE OLD PEOPLE

JOHN MONTAGUE (BORN 1929)

Like dolmens round my childhood, the old people.

Jamie MacCrystal sang to himself
A broken song, without tune, without words;
He tipped me a penny every pension day,
Fed kindly crusts to winter birds.
When he died his cottage was robbed,
Mattress and money box torn and searched,
Only the corpse they didn't disturb.

Maggie Owens was surrounded by animals,
A mongrel bitch and shivering pups,
Even in her bedroom a she-goat cried,
She was a well of gossip defiled,
Fanged chronicler of a whole countryside;
Reputed a witch, all I could find
Was her lonely need to deride.

The Nialls lived along a mountain lane
Where heather bells bloomed, clumps of foxglove.
All were blind, with Blind Pension and Wireless.
Dead eyes serpent-flickered as one entered
To shelter from a downpour of mountain rain.
Crickets chirped under the rocking hearthstone
Until the muddy sun shone out again.

Mary Moore lived in a crumbling gatehouse
Famous as Pisa for its leaning gable.
Bag apron and boots, she tramped the fields
Driving lean cattle to a miry stable.
A by-word for fierceness, she fell asleep
Over love stories, Red Star and Red Circle,
Dreamed of gypsy love rites, by firelight sealed.

Wild Billy Harbinson married a Catholic servant girl
When all his loyal family passed on:
We danced round him shouting "To hell with King Billy"
And dodged from the arc of his flailing blackthorn.
Forsaken by both creeds, he showed little concern
Until the Orange drums banged past in the summer
And bowler and sash aggressively shone.

Curate and doctor trudged to attend them,
Through knee-deep snow, through summer heat,
From main road to lane to broken path,
Gulping the mountain air with painful breath.
Sometimes they were found by neighbours,
Silent keepers of a smokeless hearth,
Suddenly cast in the mould of death.

Ancient Ireland, indeed! I was reared by her bedside,
The rune and the chant, evil eye and averted head,
Fomorian fierceness of family and local feud.
Gaunt figures of fear and of friendliness,
For years they trespassed on my dreams,
Until once, in a standing circle of stones,
I felt their shadows pass

Into that dark permanence of ancient forms.

Dolmen at Proleek, Co. Louth. 1960.
Photograph: National Parks and Monuments Branch,
Commissioners of Public Works, Ireland

YEATS AT PETITPAS by John Sloan. 1910. Oil on canvas.
In the collection of The Corcoran Gallery of Art, Washington,
D.C. Museum purchase, 1932

*Yeats's father, the artist, is pictured here,
second from left, at a favorite restaurant
during a visit to New York.*

ARE YOU CONTENT?

W. B. YEATS (1865–1939)

I call on those that call me son,
Grandson, or great-grandson,
On uncles, aunts, great-uncles or great-aunts,
To judge what I have done.
Have I, that put it into words,
Spoilt what old loins have sent?
Eyes spiritualised by death can judge,
I cannot, but I am not content.

He that in Sligo at Drumcliff
Set up the old stone Cross,
That red-headed rector in County Down,
A good man on a horse,
Sandymount Corbets, that notable man
Old William Pollexfen,
The smuggler Middleton, Butlers far back,
Half legendary men.

Infirm and aged I might stay
In some good company,
I who have always hated work,
Smiling at the sea,
Or demonstrate in my own life
What Robert Browning meant
By an old hunter talking with Gods;
But I am not content.

A SCENE IN THE PHOENIX PARK by Walter Osborne.
Late 19th century. Oil on canvas.
The National Gallery of Ireland, Dublin

SAILING TO BYZANTIUM
W. B. YEATS (1865–1939)

I

That is no country for old men. The young
In one another's arms, birds in the trees
—Those dying generations—at their song,
The salmon-falls, the mackerel-crowded seas,
Fish, flesh, or fowl, commend all summer long
Whatever is begotten, born, and dies.
Caught in that sensual music all neglect
Monuments of unageing intellect.

II

An aged man is but a paltry thing,
A tattered coat upon a stick, unless
Soul clap its hands and sing, and louder sing
For every tatter in its mortal dress,
Nor is there singing school but studying
Monuments of its own magnificence;
And therefore I have sailed the seas and come
To the holy city of Byzantium.

III

O sages standing in God's holy fire
As in the gold mosaic of a wall,
Come from the holy fire, perne in a gyre,
And be the singing-masters of my soul.
Consume my heart away; sick with desire
And fastened to a dying animal
It knows not what it is; and gather me
Into the artifice of eternity.

IV

Once out of nature I shall never take
My bodily form from any natural thing,
But such a form as Grecian goldsmiths make
Of hammered gold and gold enamelling
To keep a drowsy Emperor awake;
Or set upon a golden bough to sing
To lords and ladies of Byzantium
Of what is past, or passing, or to come.

HERITAGE
(THE VERB "TO HAVE" DOES NOT EXIST IN GAELIC)

AUGUSTUS YOUNG (BORN 1943)

(JAMES HOGAN)

One cannot possess
the house until the death
of a father, until the old man,
cutting a twist by the fire,
fails to fill the bowl,
lays down the pipe
or sometimes luckily enough
shovels himself into the earth.

One must not appear to own the place
until the first grass covers the grave.

Then you have it
and the land—one acre in ten
of arable bog. But you cannot possess
a wife until your mother
accepts the death and, in many a case,
accepts her own. There is no choice.

This is being a true son.
Allow the country die for you.

LINES IN MEMORY OF MY FATHER
BASIL PAYNE (BORN 1928)

Fishing, one morning early in July
From the canal bank—that was the closest ever
We came to entering each other's world;
That, and one wintry day at the Museum,
Looking at ancient coins and skeletons,
Dead butterflies, old guns and precious stones;
Each of us slightly awed, and slightly bored,
And slightly uneasy at each other's boredom.
I cried, of course, the morning that you died,
Frightened by Mother's tears and your grey spittle,
And frightened at being suddenly bereft
Of someone I had never loved enough,
But vaguely understood had loved me.

Today in Dublin, passing the Museum,
A dead leaf blew across my instep, stabbing
My memory suddenly: little frightened fishes
Flapping bewildered in a cheap white net,
Then gliding in a water-filled jam jar;
Nudging their awkward heads against the glass,
Groping in vain for green and spacious freedom.

FOR MY GRANDMOTHER, BRIDGET HALPIN

MICHAEL HARTNETT (BORN 1941)

maybe morning lightens over
the coldest time in all the day,
but not for you: a bird's hover,
seabird, blackbird, or bird of prey
was rain, or death, or lost cattle:
the day's warning, like red plovers
so etched and small the clouded sky,
was book to you, and true bible.
you died in utter loneliness,
your acres left to the childless.
you never saw the animals
of God, and the flower under
your feet: and the trees change a leaf:
and the red fur of a fox on
a quiet evening: and the long
birches falling down the hillside.

MAN IN RED by Patrick Harris.
1984. Oil on canvas.
Collection of An Chomhairle Ealaíon/The Arts Council, Ireland

DEATH OF AN IRISHWOMAN

MICHAEL HARTNETT (BORN 1941)

Ignorant, in the sense
she ate monotonous food
and thought the world was flat,
and pagan, in the sense
she knew the things that moved
at night were neither dogs nor cats
but púcas and darkfaced men
she nevertheless had fierce pride.
But sentenced in the end
to eat thin diminishing porridge
in a stone-cold kitchen
she clenched her brittle hands
around a world
she could not understand.
I loved her from the day she died.
She was a summer dance at the crossroads.
She was a cardgame where a nose was broken.
She was a song that nobody sings.
She was a house ransacked by soldiers.
She was a language seldom spoken.
She was a child's purse, full of useless things.

HOMECOMING

DESMOND O'GRADY (BORN 1935)

The familiar pull of the slow train
trundling after a sinking sun on shadowed fields.
White light splicing the broad span of the sky.
Evening deepens grass, the breeze,
like purple smoke, ruffles its surface.
Straight into herring-dark skies the great cathedral spire
is sheer Gothic; slender and singular,
grey as the slate at school when a child looking up—
a bottle of raspberry in one hand, a brown bag of biscuits in t'other—
Feathereye Mykie my uncle told me a man
shot down a hawk dead from the cross
with a telescope fixed to his rifle.

Pulling home now into the station. Cunneen waving
a goatskin of wine from the Spain he has never seen
like an acolyte swinging a thurible.
My father, behind him, as ever in clerical grey,
white hair shining, his hand raised,
preaching away to the Poet Ryan.
And after a drink at the White House—out home.

The house in bedlam. He's here says my father.
Sober? my mother. She's looking me over.
Bring out the bottle. Pull round the fire.
Talk of the journey, living abroad:
Paris and London, Rome and New York.
What is it like in an airplane? my sister.
Glad you could make it—my brother.
Everything here the same tuppence ha'penny—the neighbours;
just as you left it; the same old roast chestnut.
After the songs, the one for the road,
the last caller gone—up to my room.

As I used find it home for the Christmas from school.
The great brass bed. The box still under it full
of old prayerbooks, assorted mementos,
the untouched bundle of letters mottled with mould.
Now it's a house of doorways and walls
and no laughter. A place for two old people
who speak to each other but rarely. And that only
when children return. Old people mumbling
low in the night of change and of ageing
when they think you asleep and not listening—
and we wide awake in the dark,
as when we were children.

Couple at Bray, Co. Wicklow.
Photograph by Rod Tuach

Manorhamilton sheep fair, Co. Leitrim. 1981.
Photograph by Martin Parr

O COUNTRY PEOPLE

JOHN HEWITT (BORN 1907)

O country people, you of the hill farms,
huddled so in darkness I cannot tell
whether the light across the glen is a star,
or the bright lamp spilling over the sill,
I would be neighbourly, would come to terms
with your existence, but you are so far;
there is a wide bog between us, a high wall.
I've tried to learn the smaller parts of speech
in your slow language, but my thoughts need more
flexible shapes to move in, if I am to reach
into the hearth's red heart across the half-door.

You are coarse to my senses, to my washed skin;
I shall maybe learn to wear dung on my heel,
but the slow assurance, the unconscious discipline
informing your vocabulary of skill,
is beyond my mastery, who have followed a trade
three generations now, at counter and desk;
hand me a rake, and I at once, betrayed,
will shed more sweat than is needed for the task.

If I could gear my mind to the year's round,
take season into season without a break,
instead of feeling my heart bound and rebound
because of the full moon or the first snowflake,
I should have gained something. Your secret is pace.
Already in your company I can keep step,
but alone, involved in a headlong race,
I never know the moment when to stop.

I know the level you accept me on,
like a strange bird observed about the house,
or sometimes seen out flying on the moss
that may tomorrow, or next week, be gone,
liable to return without warning
on a May afternoon and away in the morning.

But we are no part of your world, your way,
as a field or a tree is, or a spring well.
We are not held to you by the mesh of kin;
we must always take a step back to begin,
and there are many things you never tell
because we would not know the things you say.

I recognize the limits I can stretch;
even a lifetime among you should leave me strange,
for I could not change enough, and you will not change;
there'd still be levels neither'd ever reach.
And so I cannot ever hope to become,
for all my goodwill toward you, yours to me,
even a phrase or a story which will come
pat to the tongue, part of the tapestry
of apt response, at the appropriate time,
like a wise saw, a joke, an ancient rime
used when the last stack's topped at the day's end,
or when the last lint's carted round the bend.

HEAD WITH LETTERS by John Kelly.
1979. Lithograph.
Collection of An Chomhairle Ealaíon/The Arts
Council, Ireland

THE TRUISMS

LOUIS MACNEICE (1907–1963)

His father gave him a box of truisms
Shaped like a coffin, then his father died;
The truisms remained on the mantelpiece
As wooden as the playbox they had been packed in
Or that other his father skulked inside.

Then he left home, left the truisms behind him
Still on the mantelpiece, met love, met war,
Sordor, disappointment, defeat, betrayal,
Till through disbeliefs he arrived at a house
He could not remember seeing before,

And he walked straight in; it was where he had come from
And something told him the way to behave.
He raised his hand and blessed his home;
The truisms flew and perched on his shoulders
And a tall tree sprouted from his father's grave.

160

FROM THE TRIADS OF IRELAND

TRANSLATED FROM THE IRISH (C. 9TH CENTURY) BY KUNO MEYER (1858–1919)

Three slender things that best support the world: the slender stream of milk from the cow's dug into the pail; the slender blade of green corn upon the ground; the slender thread over the hand of a skilled woman.

The three worst welcomes: a handicraft in the same house with the inmates; scalding water upon your feet; salt food without a drink.

Three rejoicings followed by sorrow: a wooer's, a thief's, a tale-bearer's.

Three rude ones of the world: a youngster mocking an old man; a robust person mocking an invalid; a wise man mocking a fool.

Three fair things that hide ugliness: good manners in the ill-favoured; skill in a serf; wisdom in the misshapen.

Three sparks that kindle love: a face, demeanour, speech.

Three glories of a gathering: a beautiful wife, a good horse, a swift hound.

Three fewnesses that are better than plenty: a fewness of fine words; a fewness of cows in grass; a fewness of friends around good ale.

Three ruins of a tribe: a lying chief, a false judge, a lustful priest.

Three laughing-stocks of the world: an angry man, a jealous man, a niggard.

Three signs of ill-breeding: a long visit, staring, constant questioning.

Three signs of a fop: the track of his comb in his hair; the track of his teeth in his food; the track of his stick behind him.

Three idiots of a bad guest-house: an old hag with a chronic cough; a brainless tartar of a girl; a hobgoblin of a gillie.

Three things that constitute a physician: a complete cure; leaving no blemish behind; a painless examination.

Three things betokening trouble: holding plough-land in common; performing feats together; alliance in marriage.

Three nurses of theft: a wood, a cloak, night.

Three false sisters: "perhaps," "may be," "I dare say."

Three timid brothers: "hush!" "stop!" "listen!"

Three sounds of increase: the lowing of a cow in milk; the din of a smithy; the swish of a plough.

Three steadinesses of good womanhood: keeping a steady tongue; a steady chastity; a steady housewifery.

Three excellences of dress: elegance; comfort, lastingness.

Three candles that illume every darkness: truth, nature, knowledge.

Three keys that unlock thoughts: drunkenness, trustfulness, love.

Three youthful sisters: desire, beauty, generosity.

Three aged sisters: groaning, chastity, ugliness.

Three nurses of high spirits: pride, wooing, drunkenness.

Three coffers whose depth is not known: the coffers of a chieftain, of the Church, of a privileged poet.

Three things that ruin wisdom: ignorance, inaccurate knowledge, forgetfulness.

Three things that are best for a chief: justice, peace, an army.

Three things that are worst for a chief: sloth, treachery, evil counsel.

Three services, the worst that a man can serve: serving a bad woman, a bad lord, and bad land.

Three lawful handbreadths: a handbreadth between shoes and hose, between ear and hair, and between the fringe of the tunic and the knee.

Three angry sisters: blasphemy, strife, foul-mouthedness.

Three disrespectful sisters: importunity, frivolity, flightiness.

Three signs of a bad man: bitterness, hatred, cowardice.

THE IRISH SCHOOLMASTER by E. Fitzpatrick. 19th century. Lithograph. Collection Charles Sullivan

LAMENT FOR THE WOODLANDS

TRANSLATED FROM THE IRISH (C. 17TH CENTURY)

BY FRANK O'CONNOR (1903–1966)

When once I rose at morning
The summer sun was shining,
I heard the horn awinding
    With the birds' merry songs;
There was badger and weasel,
Woodcock and plover,
And echo repeated
    The music of the guns.
The winded fox was flying,
The horsemen followed shouting,
Counting her geese on the highway
    Some woman's heart was sore;
But now the woods are falling,
We must go over the water—
Shaun O'Dwyer of the Valley
    Your pleasure is no more.

'Tis cause enough for grieving,
Our shelter felled about us,
The north wind freezing
    And death in the sky,
My merry hound tied tightly
From sporting and chasing
That would lift a young lad's sorrows
    In the noondays gone by.
The stag is on the mountain,
Swift and proud as ever,
He may come up the heather
    But our day is o'er,
Let the townsmen cease their watching
And I'll take ship from Galway,
Shaun O'Dwyer of the Valley
    Your pleasure is no more.

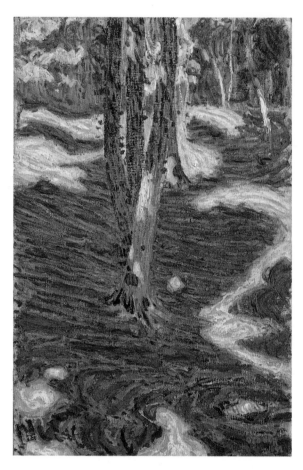

THE GLADE by Roderic O'Conor. 1892. Oil on canvas.
Collection, The Museum of Modern Art, New York.
Acquired through the Lillie P. Bliss Bequest

KILCASH
TRANSLATED FROM THE IRISH (C. 17TH CENTURY)
BY FRANK O'CONNOR (1903–1966)

What shall we do for timber?
    The last of the woods is down.
Kilcash and the house of its glory
    And the bell of the house are gone,
The spot where that lady waited
    Who shamed all women for grace
When earls came sailing to greet her
    And Mass was said in the place.

My grief and my affliction
    Your gates are taken away,
Your avenue needs attention,
    Goats in the garden stray.
The courtyard's filled with water
    And the great earls where are they?
The earls, the lady, the people
    Beaten into the clay.

No sound of duck or geese there,
    Hawk's cry or eagle's call,
No humming of the bees there
    That brought honey and wax for all,
Nor even the song of the birds there
    When the sun goes down in the west,
No cuckoo on top of the boughs there,
    Singing the world to rest.

There's mist there tumbling from branches,
    Unstirred by night and by day,
And darkness falling from heaven,
    For our fortune has ebbed away,
There's no holly nor hazel nor ash there,
    The pasture's rock and stone,
The crown of the forest has withered,
    And the last of its game is gone.

I beseech of Mary and Jesus
    That the great come home again
With long dances danced in the garden,
    Fiddle music and mirth among men,
That Kilcash the home of our fathers
    Be lifted on high again,
And from that to the deluge of waters
    In bounty and peace remain.

Kilcash Castle, Co. Tipperary. Photograph by George Mott

PAWNTICKETS

JOHN C. RYAN (BORN C.1960)

FOR MICHAEL COADY

It's hard to credit, but
in nineteen hundred and six
a brass watch
was equal to
seventeen flannel drawers;
but that was in May time
when hawthorn blossom
scented the warm breeze
off the river
and drawers were down
in value;
time, on the other hand,
seemed constant,
except in midsummer
when its marketable quality
was lost in dreaming
and there never seemed
to be an end to it;
but the solid gleam of brass
has now begun to root it
in the market place.

When hoar gleamed white
under the Townclock,
and candles lit the
faces of our fathers
clustered around cribs,
Kate Hacket's red frock
must have flamed
some December evening

before being shelved
for three and seven
beside six cotton drawers
stretched to sevenpence
on the dark counter
under the lamp.
Britches and brogues
outstripped them;
candlesticks
and canvas ticks
did not impress,
were not easily exchanged
for the price of a bottle,
a tin of snuff,
or any amount of
loaves and fishes
to fill the little dishes
down the lanes.

On a rainy September
when the mists
crowded in from
the Comeraghs
and the briars
were dreeping
with the fruits
of Autumn,
two sweep's sticks
raised enough for a smoke,
a straddle

enough to bridge the gap
between Monday and Friday,
while my grandmother
Katie Hynes
threw her shawl
on the counter
for three and a penny,
a few weeks after
the birth of my father,
unable to read the warning
that goods would be sold
in nine months time;
time to renew her interest
with another child,
time to redeem her faith
with a thousand decades
of the rosary,
a pledge or a novena
to the Sacred Heart of Jesus
for a night of song
in the back room
of Ned Drohans.

Drinkers and smokers
quiet and still;
pledger and broker
under the hill;
Christ the redeemer's
paying the bill.

164

IS THAT ALL? by Jane Morgan.
1898. Oil on canvas.
Ulster Museum, Belfast

THE COUNTY OF MAYO

TRANSLATED FROM THE IRISH (C. 19TH CENTURY)

BY GEORGE FOX (19TH CENTURY)

On the deck of Patrick Lynch's boat I sat in woeful plight,
Through my sighing all the weary day and weeping all the night.
Were it not that full of sorrow from my people forth I go,
By the blessed sun, 'tis royally I'd sing thy praise, Mayo.

When I dwelt at home in plenty, and my gold did much abound,
In the company of fair young maids the Spanish ale went round.
'Tis a bitter change from those gay days that now I'm forced to go,
And must leave my bones in Santa Cruz, far from my own Mayo.

They are altered girls in Irrul now; 'tis proud they're grown and high,
With their hair-bags and their top-knots—for I pass their buckles by.
But it's little now I heed their airs, for God will have it so,
That I must depart for foreign lands, and leave my sweet Mayo.

'Tis my grief that Patrick Loughlin is not Earl in Irrul still,
And that Brian Duff no longer rules as Lord upon the Hill;
And that Colonel Hugh McGrady should be dying dead and low,
And I sailing, sailing swiftly from the county of Mayo.

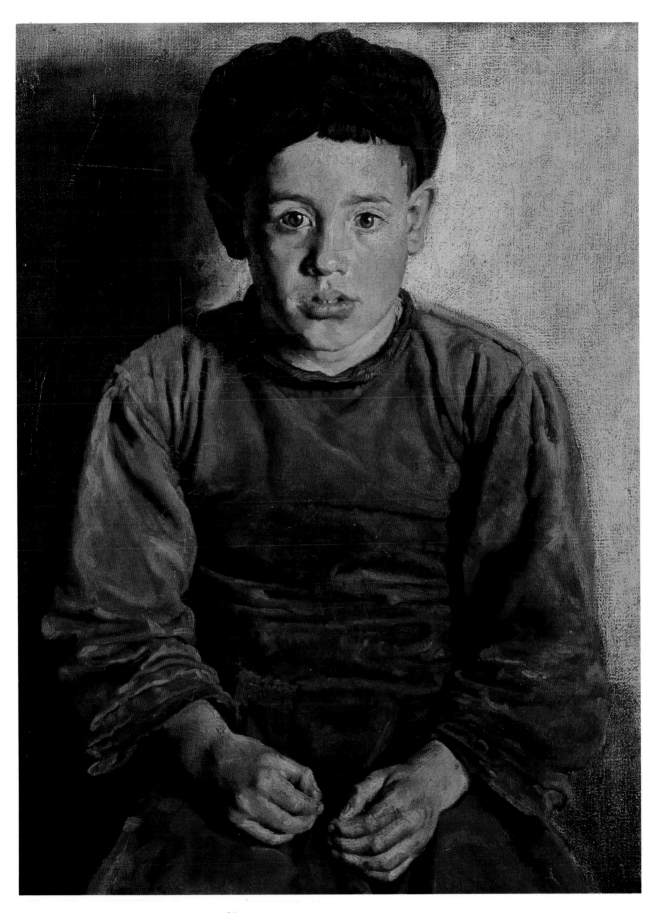

MAYO PEASANT BOY by Patrick Touhy. 1914. Oil on canvas.
The Hugh Lane Municipal Gallery of Modern Art, Dublin

WILD GEESE

(A LAMENT FOR THE IRISH JACOBITES)

KATHERINE TYNAN (1861 – 1931)

I have heard the curlew crying
  On a lonely moor and mere;
And the sea-gull's shriek in the gloaming
  Is a lonely sound in the ear:
And I've heard the brown thrush mourning
  For her children stolen away;—
But it's O for the homeless Wild Geese
  That sailed ere the dawn of day!

For the curlew out on the moorland
  Hath five fine eggs in the nest;
And the thrush will get her a new love
  And sing her song with the best.
As the swallow flies to the Summer
  Will the gull return to the sea:
But never the wings of the Wild Geese
  Will flash over seas to me.

And 'tis ill to be roaming, roaming
  With homesick heart in the breast!
And how long I've looked for your coming,
  And my heart is the empty nest!
O sore in the land of the stranger
  They'll pine for the land far away!
But day of Aughrim, my sorrow,
  It was you was the bitter day!

LAST LINES

EGAN O RAHILLY (1670–1728)

TRANSLATED FROM THE IRISH BY FRANK O'CONNOR (1903–1966)

I shall not call for help until they coffin me—
    What good for me to call when hope of help is gone?
Princes of Munster who would have heard my cry
    Will not rise from the dead because I am alone.

Mind shudders like a wave in this tempestuous mood,
    My bowels and my heart are pierced and filled with pain
To see our lands, our hills, our gentle neighborhood
    A plot where any English upstart stakes his claim.

The Shannon and the Liffey and the tuneful Lee,
    The Boyne and the Blackwater a sad music sing,
The waters of the west run red into the sea—
    No matter what be trumps, their knave will beat our king.

And I can never cease weeping these useless tears;
    I am a man oppressed, afflicted and undone
Who where he wanders mourning no companion hears
    Only some waterfall that has no cause to mourn.

Now I shall cease, death comes, and I must not delay
    By Laune and Laine and Lee, diminished of their pride,
I shall go after the heroes, ay, into the clay—
    My fathers followed theirs before Christ was crucified.

LEAVING INISHMORE

MICHAEL LONGLEY (BORN 1939)

Rain and sunlight and the boat between them
Shifted whole hillsides through the afternoon—
Quiet variations on an urgent theme
Reminding me now that we left too soon
The island awash in wave and anthem.

Miles from the brimming enclave of the bay
I hear again the Atlantic's voices,
The gulls above us as we pulled away—
So munificent their final noises
These are the broadcasts from our holiday.

Oh, the crooked walkers on that tilting floor!
And the girls singing on the upper deck
Whose hair took the light like a downpour—
Interim nor change of scene shall shipwreck
Those folk on the move between shore and shore.

Summer and solstice as the seasons turn
Anchor our boat in a perfect standstill,
The harbour wall of Inishmore astern
Where the Atlantic waters overspill—
I shall name this the point of no return

Lest that excursion out of light and heat
Take on a January idiom—
Our ocean icebound when the year is hurt,
Wintertime past cure—the curriculum
Vitae of sailors and the sick at heart.

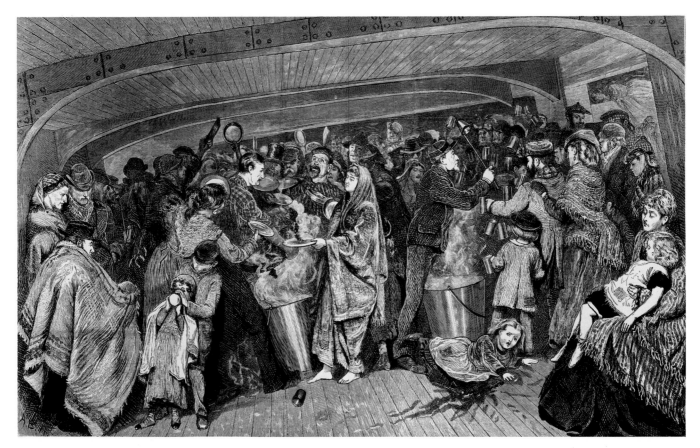

BETWEEN DECKS ON AN EMIGRANT SHIP—FEEDING TIME: A SKETCH FROM LIFE by A. B. Houghton.
1870. Engraving. The Metropolitan Museum of Art, New York

THE BATTERY, THE BAY AND HARBOR OF NEW YORK by Samuel Waugh. 1855. Watercolor on canvas.
Museum of the City of New York

IRELAND

DORA SIGERSON (1866–1918)

'Twas the dream of a God,
  And the mould of His hand,
That you shook 'neath His stroke,
That you trembled and broke
  To this beautiful land.

Here He loosed from His hold
  A brown tumult of wings,
Till the wind on the sea
Bore the strange melody
  Of an island that sings.

He made you all fair,
  You in purple and gold,
You in silver and green,
Till no eye that has seen
  Without love can behold.

I have left you behind
  In the path of the past,
With the white breath of flowers,
With the best of God's hours,
  I have left you at last.

WOODS

LOUIS MACNEICE (1907–1963)

My father who found the English landscape tame
Had hardly in his life walked in a wood,
Too old when first he met one; Malory's knights,
Keats's nymphs or the Midsummer Night's Dream
Could never arras the room, where he spelled out
   True and Good
With their interleaving of half-truths and not-quites.

While for me from the age of ten the socketed
   wooden gate
Into a Dorset planting, into a dark
But gentle ambush, was an alluring eye;
Within was a kingdom free from time and sky,
Caterpillar webs on the forehead, danger under the feet,
And the mind adrift in a floating and rustling ark

Packed with birds and ghosts, two of every race,
Trills of love from the picture-book—Oh might I never
   land
But here, grown six foot tall, find me also a love
Also out of the picture-book; whose hand
Would be soft as the webs of the wood and on her face
The wood-pigeon's voice would shaft a chrism from
   above.

So in a grassy ride a rain-filled hoof-mark coined
By a finger of sun from the mint of Long Ago

Was the last of Lancelot's glitter. Make-believe dies hard;
That the rider passed here lately and is a man we know
Is still untrue, the gate to Legend remains unbarred,
The grown-up hates to divorce what the child joined.

Thus from a city when my father would frame
Escape, he thought, as I do, of bog or rock
But I have also this other, this English, choice
Into what yet is foreign; whatever its name
Each wood is the mystery and the recurring shock
Of its dark coolness is a foreign voice.

Yet in using the word tame my father was maybe right,
These woods are not the Forest; each is moored
To a village somewhere near. If not of today
They are not like the wilds of Mayo, they are assured
Of their place by men; reprieved from the neolithic
   night
By gamekeepers or by Herrick's girls at play.

And always we walk out again. The patch
Of sky at the end of the path grows and discloses
An ordered open air long ruled by dyke and fence,
With geese whose form and gait proclaim their
   consequence,
Pargetted outposts, windows browed with thatch,
And cow pats—and inconsequent wild roses.

AN IRISHMAN IN COVENTRY

JOHN HEWITT (BORN 1907)

A full year since, I took this eager city,
the tolerance that laced its blatant roar,
its famous steeples and its web of girders,
as image of the state hope argued for,
and scarcely flung a bitter thought behind me
on all that flaws the glory and the grace
which ribbons through the sick, guilt-clotted legend
of my creed-haunted, Godforsaken race.
My rhetoric swung round from steel's high promise
to the precision of the well-gauged tool,
tracing the logic in the vast glass headlands,
the clockwork horse, the comprehensive school.

Then, sudden, by occasion's chance concerted,
in enclave of my nation, but apart,
the jigging dances and the lilting fiddle
stirred the old rage and pity in my heart.
The faces and the voices blurring round me,
the strong hands long familiar with the spade,
the whiskey-tinctured breath, the pious buttons,
called up a people endlessly betrayed
by our own weakness, by the wrongs we suffered
in that long twilight over bog and glen,
by force, by famine and by glittering fables
which gave us martyrs when we needed men,
by faith which had no charity to offer,
by poisoned memory and by ready wit,
with poverty corroded into malice
to hit and run and howl when it is hit.

This is our fate: eight hundred years' disaster
crazily tangled as the Book of Kells,
the dream's distortion and the land's division,
the midnight raiders and the prison cells.
Yet like Lir's children banished to the waters
our hearts still listen for the landward bells.

IMMIGRANT DAUGHTER'S SONG
MARY ANN LARKIN (BORN 1945)

All gone,
the silver-green silk of time
winding down centuries
of custom and kinship
the pouring of the sea
the stars, bright pictures
on the slate of night,
the moon stamping forever
the spire of the church
on the sand,
bird-song, wind-song, mother-song
Even time itself changed
to a ticking, a dot on a line

Customs of grace and gentleness gone
name-saying
and knowing
who begat who
and when and where
and who could work
and who could sing
and who would pray
and who would not
and where the fish ran
and the wild plums hid
and how the old mothers
fit their babies' fingers
to the five-flowered hollows
of blue ladyfingers
And whose father fought whose
with golden swords
a thousand years ago
at Ballyferriter
on the strand below the church

All gone
changed from a silken spool unwinding
to rooms of relics and loss
behind whose locked doors
I dream
not daring to wake

THE FAIR GERALDINE by the Master of the Countess of Warwick.
17th century. Oil on panel.
The National Gallery of Ireland, Dublin

The name "Geraldine" refers to the Fitzgerald family.

The Countes of Lincolne
The Faire Geraldina
Celebrated in the Verse of
Surrey Poems

OLD IRELAND

WALT WHITMAN (1819–1892)

Far hence amid an isle of wondrous beauty,

Crouching over a grave an ancient sorrowful mother,

Once a queen, now lean and tatter'd seated on the ground,

Her old white hair drooping dishevel'd round her shoulders,

At her feet fallen an unused royal harp,

Long silent, she too long silent, mourning her shrouded hope and heir,

Of all the earth her heart most full of sorrow because most full of love.

Yet a word ancient mother,

You need crouch there no longer on the cold ground with forehead
    between your knees,

O you need not sit there veil'd in your old white hair so dishevel'd,

For know you the one you mourn is not in that grave,

It was an illusion, the son you love was not really dead,

The Lord is not dead, he is risen again young and strong in another
    country,

Even while you wept there by your fallen harp by the grave,

What you wept for was translated, pass'd from the grave,

The winds favor'd and the sea sail'd it,

And now with rosy and new blood,

Moves to-day in a new country.

A TIME FOR GREATNESS—KENNEDY AT NOMINATING CONVENTION
by Norman Rockwell. Lithograph. Cover for LOOK magazine, 14 July 1964

SPENSER'S IRELAND

MARIANNE MOORE (1887–1972)

has not altered;—
   a place as kind as it is green,
   the greenest place I've never seen.
Every name is a tune.
Denunciations do not affect
    the culprit; nor blows, but it
is torture to him to not be spoken to.
They're natural—
    the coat, like Venus'
mantle lined with stars,
buttoned close at the neck—the sleeves new from disuse.

If in Ireland
   they play the harp backward at need,
   and gather at midday the seed
of the fern, eluding
their "giants all covered with iron," might
    there be fern seed for unlearn-
ing obduracy and for reinstating
the enchantment?
    Hindered characters
seldom have mothers
in Irish stories, but they all have grandmothers.

It was Irish;
   a match not a marriage was made
   when my great great grandmother'd said
with native genius for
disunion, "Although your suitor be
   perfection, one objection
is enough; he is not
Irish." Outwitting
    the fairies, befriending the furies,
whoever again
and again says, "I'll never give in," never sees

that you're not free
   until you've been made captive by
   supreme belief—credulity
you say? When large dainty
fingers tremblingly divide the wings
    of the fly for mid-July
with a needle and wrap it with peacock tail,
or tie wool and
    buzzard's wing, their pride,
like the enchanter's
is in care, not madness. Concurring hands divide

flax for damask
   that when bleached by Irish weather
   has the silvered chamois-leather
water-tightness of a
skin. Twisted torcs and gold new-moon-shaped
    lunulae aren't jewelry
like the purple-coral fuchsia-tree's. Eire—
the guillemot
    so neat and the hen
of the heath and the
linnet spinet-sweet—bespeak relentlessness? Then

they are to me
   like enchanted Earl Gerald who
   changed himself into a stag, to
a great green-eyed cat of
the mountain. Discommodity makes
    them invisible; they've dis-
appeared. The Irish say your trouble is their
trouble and your
    joy their joy? I wish
I could believe it;
I am troubled, I'm dissatisfied, I'm Irish.

Ruins of Kilcolman Castle, Co. Cork. Photograph by George Mott

This was the home of the English poet Edmund Spenser during his stay in Ireland, 1586–98.

INSIDE THE HOUSE IS WARM
FROM NIGHTFALL, MIDWINTER, MISSOURI

BRIAN COFFEY (BORN 1905)

Inside the house is warm.
Winter outside blows from Canada
freezing rain to ice our trees
branch by branch, leaf by leaf.
The mare shelters in the barn.

On the impassable road no movement.
Nothing stirs in the sky against the black.
If memory were an ice-field
quiet as all outside!
Tonight the poetry is in the children's game:
I am distracted by comparisons,
Ireland across the grey ocean,
here, across the wide river. . . .

We live far from where
my mother grows very old.
Five miles away, at Byrnesville,
the cemetery is filled with Irish graves,
the priest an old man born near Cork,
his bloss like the day he left the land.

People drifted in here from the river,
Irish, German, Bohemians,
more than one hundred years ago,
come to make homes.

Many Irish souls have gone back to God
from Byrnesville,

many are Irish here today
where cedars stand like milestones
on worn Ozark hills
and houses white on bluegrass lawns
house people honest, practical and kind.

All shows to a long love
yet I am charmed
by the hills behind Dublin,
those white stone cottages,
grass green as no other green is green,
my mother's people, their ways.

France one loves with a love apart
like the love of wisdom;
Of England everyday love is the true love;
there is a love of Ireland
withering for Irishmen.

Does it matter where one dies,
supposing one knows how?

NAMES

GERALD DAWE (BORN 1952)

They call this "Black North"
black from the heart out—

it doesn't matter about
particularities when mouths

mumble the handy sayings
and day-in minds tighten.

I've been here having thought
nowhere else was possible,

a condition of destiny or what
the old generations only fumbled

with: conceit, success, a fair
share of decent hardship,

compounded, forced into fierce
recognition—the cardhouse toppled.

In this extreme, perched
on the edge of the Atlantic

you feel to look down
and gather around the details

thinking to store them away
bundle and pack in the exile's way—

the faithful journey
of turning your back

like the host of others
the scholars and saints.

Line up and through the turn-
stile, click the ticket

and wait till you're
clear of it: glued to

the passport: IRISH POET,
Destination, America or

Early Grave. You need never
recall the other names.

THE IRISH TROUBLES by Robert Motherwell. 1981.
Acrylic and collage on canvas board.
Courtesy Mrs. Hugo V. Neuhaus, Jr.

American woman at the British Embassy in Washington, D.C.,
protesting British policy toward Ireland in December 1920.
Photograph. National Library of Ireland, Dublin

ANTRIM

ROBINSON JEFFERS (1887–1962)

No spot of earth where men have so fiercely for ages of time
Fought and survived and cancelled each other,
Pict and Gael and Dane, McQuillan, Clandonnel, O'Neill,
Savages, the Scot, the Norman, the English,
Here in the narrow passage and the pitiless north, perpetual
Betrayals, relentless resultless fighting.
A random fury of dirks in the dark: a struggle for survival
Of hungry blind cells of life in the womb.
But now the womb has grown old, her strength has gone forth; a few
   red carts in a fog creak flax to the dubs,
And sheep in the high heather cry hungrily that life is hard; a
   plaintive peace; shepherds and peasants.

We have felt the blades meet in the flesh in a hundred ambushes
And the groaning blood bubble in the throat;
In a hundred battles the heavy axes bite the deep bone,
The mountain suddenly stagger and be darkened.
Generation on generation we have seen the blood of boys
And heard the moaning of women massacred,
The passionate flesh and nerves have flamed like pitch-pine and fallen
And lain in the earth softly dissolving.
I have lain and been humbled in all these graves, and mixed new flesh
   with the old and filled the hollow of my mouth
With maggots and rotten dust and ages of repose. I lie here and plot
   the agony of resurrection.

RIGHT OF WAY
EUGENE MCCARTHY (BORN 1916)

Here you find no counted seeds
Or calculated crops
Only the most wanted weeds
Nettles, great thistles, and burdocks
With exiles and expatriates from pot and box
Gypsy plants, despising rows
Alien corn, unhelped by hoes
Asters, lupine, sumac, and thorn—
Stranger plants, of no fame,
Which country Adams across
the fence, look at
As of forbidden knowledge
And refuse to name

Free and not free
In this sanctuary
I reached, seeking you, in want
All the joints of my arm parted
And then drew back a hand
Bled by the rasp of harsh grass
With a reed made
of that bitter blade
I blew three notes
And thought of how
If you were there
I would hold your hair
Against the wind, and hear through it
The harping of all the wild songs
Of Ireland.

ANOTHER KIND OF COUNTRY

CHARLES SULLIVAN (BORN 1933)

He could see things
invisible to me
in any kind of country
that he found—once
when the river was still
unfamiliar, he asked me why
the sky had run aground, but
looking past him, I could only see
a man, a boy, not unlike us
yet most unlike, their posture
softened by the underwater light,
their wishes sure to be fulfilled
until the fish explored their heads
and read their minds.

Then the question blew away,
and I was in another kind
of country, I could see things
invisible to him that blinded me—
his mother's imitation of a smile,
her hazel eyes enraged while she
denied it, the clothes she wore
an accusation of a crime for which
the sentences are taking too much time.

Now I climb the same uneven stairs,
remembering the words, the other things
we couldn't find together. Somehow
as I tried to see flamingoes cross
our covered bridge, she became invisible
to me, somewhere in the shadow of that ridge
I lost her love. Whatever might have been,
this was not her country, and despite
the shining promise of a few old farms
at night, it isn't mine. I'm getting cold
beside the window, tired of looking out.

My son has seen more winter nights
than this on his computer screen,
and so he writes the universal colors
of such music as the dead rehearse
for skulls and heads and nimble bones
to dance to. He's alone behind his mask,
he wouldn't answer if I asked him
how to find a country of astounding
elephants, or Irish castles rising
over ordinary towns, or traces
of young robin hoods with snowflakes
on their faces, riding slowly
through the woods beyond our house.

U2.
Photograph ©
Anton Corbijn,
1984

Irish rock group near castle ruins.

IRISH LULLABY

ALFRED PERCIVAL GRAVES (1846 – 1931)

I'd rock my own sweet childie to rest in a cradle of gold on a bough of the willow,
To the shoheen ho of the wind of the west and the lulla lo of the soft sea billow.
      Sleep, baby dear,
      Sleep without fear,
   Mother is here beside your pillow.

I'd put my own sweet childie to sleep in a silver boat on the beautiful river,
Where a shoheen whisper the white cascades, and a lulla lo the green flags shiver.
      Sleep, baby dear,
      Sleep without fear,
   Mother is here with you for ever.

Lulla lo! to the rise and fall of mother's bosom 'tis sleep has bound you,
And O, my child, what cosier nest for rosier rest could love have found you?
      Sleep, baby dear,
      Sleep without fear,
   Mother's two arms are clasped around you.

A CHRISTMAS CHILDHOOD

PATRICK KAVANAGH (1904–1967)

I

One side of the potato-pits was white with frost—
How wonderful that was, how wonderful!
And when we put our ears to the paling-post
The music that came out was magical.

The light between the ricks of hay and straw
Was a hole in Heaven's gable. An apple tree
With its December-glinting fruit we saw—
O you, Eve, were the world that tempted me

To eat the knowledge that grew in clay
And death the germ within it! Now and then
I can remember something of the gay
Garden that was childhood's. Again

The tracks of cattle to a drinking-place,
A green stone lying sideways in a ditch
Or any common sight the transfigured face
Of a beauty that the world did not touch.

II

My father played the melodeon
Outside at our gate;
There were stars in the morning east
And they danced to his music.

Across the wild bogs his melodeon called
To Lennons and Callans.
As I pulled on my trousers in a hurry
I knew some strange thing had happened.

Outside in the cow-house my mother
Made the music of milking;
The light of her stable-lamp was a star
And the frost of Bethlehem made it twinkle.

A water-hen screeched in the bog,
Mass-going feet
Crunched the wafer-ice on the pot-holes,
Somebody wistfully twisted the bellows wheel.

My child poet picked out the letters
On the grey stone,
In silver the wonder of a Christmas townland,
The winking glitter of a frosty dawn.

Cassiopeia was over
Cassidy's hanging hill,
I looked and three whin bushes rode across
The horizon—the Three Wise Kings.

An old man passing said:
"Can't he make it talk"—
The melodeon. I hid in the doorway
And tightened the belt of my box-pleated coat.

I nicked six nicks on the door-post
With my penknife's big blade—
There was a little one for cutting tobacco.
And I was six Christmases of age.

My father played the melodeon,
My mother milked the cows,
And I had a prayer like a white rose pinned
On the Virgin Mary's blouse.

CLIONA

CATHERINE TWOMEY (BORN C.1960)

FOR CLAIRE

You are letting her go
from you slowly
so gently she hardly
knows.
She unties you like
an apron,
puts you on again.
Watching her grow
is catching yourself
after years, hearing
your own voice.

In sunlight
she returns to you
from her swim
to be dried.

Little fish.
You remember the bowl
of your womb, the ocean
that held her where
you felt her swim.

You are letting her out
now, loosening
like a kite's string
seeing her for the first
time in her own orbit
in the drive, cycling.

ODE

ARTHUR O'SHAUGHNESSY (1844–1881)

We are the music-makers
   And we are the dreamers of dreams,
Wandering by lone sea-breakers,
   And sitting by desolate streams;—
World-losers and world-forsakers,
   On whom the pale moon gleams:
Yet we are the movers and shakers
   Of the world for ever, it seems.

With wonderful deathless ditties
We build up the world's great cities,
   And out of a fabulous story
   We fashion an empire's glory:
One man with a dream, at pleasure,
   Shall go forth and conquer a crown;
And three with a new song's measure
   Can trample an empire down.

We, in the ages lying
   In the buried past of the earth,
Built Nineveh with our sighing,
   And Babel itself with our mirth;
And o'erthrew them with prophesying,
   To the old of the new world's worth;
For each age is a dream that is dying,
   Or one that is coming to birth.

MIDDAY ON THE BEACH by William Orpen. 1910. Oil on canvas.
Private collection, Ireland

DIAMOND PLAN, NORTHERN IRON by Evelyn Montague. c. 1987.
Mixed fabrics, machine-pieced and hand-quilted

MOUNT EAGLE

JOHN MONTAGUE (BORN 1929)

1

The eagle looked at this changing world;
sighed and disappeared into the mountain.

Before he left he had a last reconnoitre:
the multi-coloured boats in the harbour

nodded their masts and a sandy white
crescent of strand smiled back at him.

How he liked the slight, drunk lurch
of the fishing fleet, the tide hoist-

ing them a little, at their ropes' end.
Beyond, wrack, and the jutting rocks

emerging, slowly, monsters stained
and slimed with strands of seaweed.

Ashore, beached boats and lobster-
pots, settled as hens in the sand.

2

Content was life in its easiest form;
another was the sudden growling storm

which the brooding eagle preferred,
bending his huge wings into the winds'

wild buffeting, or thrusting down along
the wide sky, at an angle, slideways

to survey the boats, scurrying homewards,
tacking against the now contrary winds,

all of whom he knew by their names.
To be angry in the morning, calmed

by midday, but brooding again in
the evening was all in a day's quirk

with lengthy intervals for silence,
gliding along, like a blessing, while

the fleet toiled on earnestly beneath
him, bulging with a fine day's catch.

3

But now he had to enter the mountain.
Why? Because a cliff had asked him?

The whole world was changing, with one
language dying; and another encroaching,

bright with buckets, cries of children.
There seemed to be no end to them,

and the region needed a guardian—
so the mountain had told him. And

a different destiny lay before him:
to be the spirit of that mountain.

Everyone would stand in awe of him.
When he was wrapped in the mist's caul

they would withdraw because of him,
peer from behind blind or curtain.

When he lifted his wide forehead
bold with light, in the morning,

they would all laugh and smile with him.
It was a greater task than an eagle's

aloofness, but sometimes, under his oilskin
of coiled mist, he sighs for lost freedom.

GLENGORMLEY

DEREK MAHON (BORN 1941)

FOR PADRAIC FIACC

Wonders are many and none is more wonderful than man
Who has tamed the terrier, trimmed the hedge
And grasped the principle of the watering can.
Clothes-pegs litter the window-ledge
And the long ships lie in clover. Washing lines
Shake out white linen over the chalk thanes.

Now we are safe from monsters, and the giants
Who tore up sods twelve miles by six
And hurled them out to sea to become islands
Can worry us no more. The sticks
And stones that once broke bones will not now harm
A generation of such sense and charm.

Only words hurt us now. No saint or hero,
Landing at night from the conspiring seas,
Brings dangerous tokens to the new era—
Their sad names linger in the histories.
The unreconciled, in their metaphysical pain,
Strangle on lamp-posts in the dawn rain

And much dies with them. I should rather praise
A worldly time under this worldly sky—
The terrier-taming, garden-watering days
Those heroes pictured as they struggled through
The quick noose of their finite being. By
Necessity, if not choice, I live here too.

IRISH TIMES by Peter David Morgan. 1987. Mixed media.
Collection of the artist

ON BEHALF OF SOME IRISHMEN NOT FOLLOWERS OF TRADITION

AE (GEORGE RUSSELL) (1867 – 1935)

They call us aliens, we are told,
Because our wayward visions stray
From that dim banner they unfold,
The dreams of worn-out yesterday.
The sum of all the past is theirs,
The creeds, the deeds, the fame, the name,
Whose death-created glory flares
And dims the spark of living flame.
They weave the necromancer's spell,
And burst the graves where martyrs slept,
Their ancient story to retell,
Renewing tears the dead have wept.
And they would have us join their dirge,
This worship of an extinct fire
In which they drift beyond the verge
Where races all outworn expire.
The worship of the dead is not
A worship that our hearts allow,
Though every famous shade were wrought
With woven thorns above the brow.
We fling our answer back in scorn:
"We are less children of this clime
Than of some nation yet unborn
Or empire in the womb of time.
We hold the Ireland in the heart
More than the land our eyes have seen,
And love the goal for which we start
More than the tale of what has been."
The generations as they rise
May live the life men lived before,
Still hold the thought once held as wise,
Go in and out by the same door.
We leave the easy peace it brings:
The few we are shall still unite
In fealty to unseen kings
Or unimaginable light.
We would no Irish sign efface,
But yet our lips would gladlier hail
The firstborn of the Coming Race
Than the last splendour of the Gael.
No blazoned banner we unfold—
One charge alone we give to youth,
Against the sceptred myth to hold
The golden heresy of truth.

GOLD PAINTING 33
by Patrick Scott. 1965. Gold leaf and tempera on canvas.
Collection The Bank of Ireland

Farm scene, Achill Island.
Photograph by Richard Fitzgerald

PEACE

PATRICK KAVANAGH (1904–1967)

And sometimes I am sorry when the grass
Is growing over the stones in quiet hollows
And the cocksfoot leans across the rutted cart-pass
That I am not the voice of country fellows
Who now are standing by some headland talking
Of turnips and potatoes or young corn
Or turf banks stripped for victory.
Here Peace is still hawking
His coloured combs and scarves and beads of horn.

Upon a headland by a whiny hedge
A hare sits looking down a leaf-lapped furrow,
There's an old plough upside-down on a weedy ridge
And someone is shouldering home a saddle-harrow.
Out of that childhood country what fools climb
To fight with tyrants Love and Life and Time?

PROSPECT
LOUIS MACNEICE (1907–1963)

Though loves languish and sour
Fruit puts the teeth on edge,
Though the ragged nests are empty of song
In the barbed and blistered hedge,

Though old men's lives and children's bricks
Spell out a Machiavellian creed,
Though the evil Past is ever present
And the happy Present is past indeed,

Though the stone grows and grows
That we roll up the hill
And the hill grows and grows
And gravity conquers still,

Though Nature's laws exploit
And defeat anarchic men,
Though every sandcastle concept
Being *ad hoc* must crumble again,

And though to-day is arid,
We know—and knowing bless—
That rooted in futurity
There is a plant of tenderness.

Girl in the west of Ireland.
Photograph by Jill Uris

DOVE 1 by Conor Fallon. 1979. Steel.
Collection The College of Music, Dublin

A NATION ONCE AGAIN

THOMAS DAVIS (1814–1845)

When boyhood's fire was in my blood,
   I read of ancient freemen,
For Greece and Rome who bravely stood,
   Three Hundred men and Three men.
And then I prayed I yet might see
   Our fetters rent in twain,
And Ireland, long a province, be
   A Nation once again.

And, from that time, through wildest woe,
   That hope has shone, a far light;
Nor could love's brightest summer glow
   Outshine that solemn starlight:
It seemed to watch above my head
   In forum, field, and fane;
Its angel voice sang round my bed,
   "A Nation once again."

It whispered, too, that "freedom's ark
   And service high and holy,
Would be profaned by feelings dark,
   And passions vain or lowly;
For freedom comes from God's right hand,
   And needs a godly train;
And righteous men must make our land
   A Nation once again."

So, as I grew from boy to man,
   I bent me to that bidding—
My spirit of each selfish plan
   And cruel passion ridding;
For, thus I hoped some day to aid—
   Oh! can such hope be vain?
When my dear country shall be made
   A Nation once again.

AE (GEORGE RUSSELL) (1867–1935). Born in Lurgan, Co. Armagh, died in Bournemouth. Writer, painter, mystic; helped to launch the "Irish Renaissance" in the late 19th century, deeply influenced Yeats and other poets. Books include *Collected Poems* (1913) and *House of Titans* (1934).

AUDEN, W. H. (1907–1963). Poet and playwright; born in England, became an American citizen in 1946. Taught at Swarthmore College, Pennsylvania, and elsewhere. Awarded the Pulitzer Prize in 1948.

BECKETT, SAMUEL (1906–1989). Poet, novelist, and playwright; born in Dublin, moved to Paris in the 1930s. Best known for *Waiting for Godot* (1952) and other plays. Awarded the Nobel Prize for Literature in 1969. *Collected Poems in English and French* published in 1977.

BOLAND, EAVAN (Born 1945). Poet and critic, born in Dublin; her books of verse include *New Territory* (1967), *The War Horse* (1975), *In Her Own Image* (1980), and *Night Feed* (1983).

BUCHANAN, GEORGE (Born 1904). Born in Co. Antrim, he worked as a journalist for the London *Times* and other newspapers before joining the RAF in 1940. Prolific novelist, essayist, and playwright. Poetry books include *Conversation with Strangers* (1961) and *Inside Traffic* (1976).

BURNS, ROBERT (1759–1796). Scottish poet and lyricist whose best-known verses, such as "Auld Lang Syne" and "Coming thro' the Rye," were written in dialect. His poem "The Farewell" is about soldiers sent from Scotland to fight in Ireland during the 17th century.

CARSON, CIARAN (Born 1948). Poet, born in Belfast, who became a teacher and civil servant with the Arts Council of Northern Ireland. His book *The New Estate* was published in 1976.

CLARKE, AUSTIN (NÉ AUGUSTINE JOSEPH) (1896–1974). Poet, novelist, dramatist, and critic. Lived for many years near Dublin and printed much of his poetry on a handpress. *Collected Poems* published in 1974.

CLIFFORD, SIGERSON (1913–1985). Born in Cork, died in Dublin. Author of *Ballads of a Bogman* (1955), he also wrote several plays, including *The Wild Colonial Boy* and *The Great Pacificator,* produced by the Abbey Theatre in 1947.

COCHRANE, SHIRLEY GRAVES (Born 1939). American poet and teacher who lives in Washington, D.C. Her published work includes *Families and Other Strangers* (1986).

COFFEY, BRIAN (Born 1905). Poet, born in Dublin, who was a member of James Joyce's circle in Paris during the 1930s. His books include *Dice Thrown Never Will Annul Chance* (1961) and *Death of Hektor* (1984).

COLUM, PADRAIC (1881–1972). Born in Co. Longford, died in Connecticut. One of the first Abbey playwrights, also wrote poetry and novels about Ireland, including *The Flying Swans* (1957). Spent much of his later life in America working for publishers and lecturing.

DAVIS, THOMAS (1814–1845). A leader of the Young Ireland political party and one of the founders of a patriotic newspaper, *The Nation*, in 1842; wrote nationalistic articles and poems that strongly influenced his contemporaries.

DAWE, GERALD (Born 1952). Poet, essayist, playwright, editor; born in Belfast, teaches at University College, Galway. His poetry books include *Sheltering Places* (1978) and *The Younger Irish Poets* (1985), an anthology.

DEANE, SEAMUS (Born 1940). Poet and essayist, born in Derry; now professor at University College, Dublin. Has published *Gradual Wars* (1972) and *History Lessons* (1983), among other books of poetry.

DE VERE, SIR AUBREY (1788–1846). A progressive and humane landlord, who was born and died at Curragh Chase, the family estate near Adare. Wrote all kinds of poetry, including sonnets that Wordsworth described as "the most perfect of our age."

DEVLIN, DENIS (1908–1959). Born in Scotland, educated in France, rose in the diplomatic service to become Ireland's ambassador to Italy in 1950. His books of verse, starting with *Intercessions* (1937), attracted the attention of Robert Penn Warren and other American poets.

DONNELLY, CHARLES (1910–1937). Born in Co. Tyrone; killed in action with the Abraham Lincoln Brigade at Jarama, Spain. His poetry was not collected during his lifetime.

DOWDEN, EDWARD (1843–1913). Born in Cork; professor at Trinity College, Dublin; authority on Shakespeare and Shelley.

FALLON, PADRAIC (1906–1974). Author, civil servant, farmer who lived mostly in Co. Wexford; wrote successful radio plays and verse dramas about Irish legends, but resisted having his shorter poetry published in book form until *Poems* (1973).

FERGUSON, SIR SAMUEL (1810–1886). Born in Belfast, died in Dublin. Lawyer and politician who later gained fame as poet and expert on Ogham inscriptions and other Irish antiquities. Knighted in 1878 for his public services.

FIACC, PADRAIC (PATRICK JOSEPH O'CONNOR) (Born 1924). Born in Belfast, lived with his parents in New York before returning to Northern Ireland in 1946. Books include *By the Black Stream* (1969) and *Nights in the Bad Place* (1977).

FOX, GEORGE (19th cent.). A virtually unknown Irish poet who graduated from Trinity College, Dublin, in 1847 and went to America in 1848. According to *Irish Minstrelsy* (1887) he wrote "some sympathetic and scholarly translations from the Celtic."

GOLDSMITH, OLIVER (1728–1774). Born in Co. Longford, died in London; wrote novels, such as *The Vicar of Wakefield* (1766), and comedies, including *She Stoops to Conquer* (1773), but his long poem "The Deserted Village" (1770) recalls an earlier and sadder period of Irish history.

GRAVES, ALFRED PERCIVAL (1846–1931). Writer and editor, born in Dublin, who enjoyed life greatly. His son Robert said, "He could dance a jig to the end."

HARDWICK, NATALIE (Born c. 1975). One of the talented schoolchildren whose writing has been published in *Being Young in Northern Ireland* (1988).

HARTNETT, MICHAEL (Born 1941). Poet and lecturer, born in Limerick; books include *Hag of Beare* (1969), *Prisoners* (1977), and *Collected Poems in English* (1984).

HAYES, DANIEL (18th cent.). Wrote about the notorious Hell Fire Club of Limerick; his *Works in Verse* were published in London, 1769. An epitaph, undated, in St. Mary's Cathedral, Limerick, says: "Dan Hayes, an honest man and a lover of his country." This may be a good example of Irish humor if it's the same Hayes.

HEANEY, SEAMUS (Born 1939). Born in Co. Derry. Poet, winner of numerous awards, distinguished professor at Harvard University; books include *Death of a Naturalist* (1966), *Bog Poems* (1975), and *Station Island* (1984).

HEWITT, JOHN (Born 1907). Born in Belfast. Poet, critic,

and museum official in Belfast and Coventry. Books of poetry include *No Rebel Word* (1948), *Out of My Time* (1974), *The Rain Dance* (1978), and *Mosaic* (1982).

HUGHES, TED (NÉ EDWARD J.) (Born 1930). Winner of many awards and author of poetry books, including *The Hawk in the Rain* (1967), *Crow* (1970), *Season Songs* (1976), *Under the North Star* (1981), and *Flowers and Insects* (1987). Since 1984 the British Poet Laureate.

HYDE, DOUGLAS (1860–1949). Author and statesman. Born in Sligo, devoted his life to restoration of Irish language and culture; founded the Gaelic League in 1893; first president of Ireland, 1937.

INGRAM, JOHN KELLS (1823–1907). Born in Newry, Co. Down; author, professor, and President of the Royal Irish Academy. Books include *A History of Political Economy* (1888) and *Practical Morals* (1904).

JEFFERS, ROBINSON (1887–1962). American poet who celebrated California's Big Sur and other scenic places. On the rugged edge of the Pacific, he built and inhabited a tower not unlike those along the Irish coast.

JOYCE, JAMES (1882–1941). Born in Dublin, died in Zurich. Gained fame as a writer of short stories with *Dubliners* (1914), but best known for his novels: *A Portrait of the Artist as a Young Man* (1916), *Ulysses* (1922), and *Finnegans Wake* (1939).

KAVANAGH, PATRICK (1904–1967). Born in Co. Monaghan, lived for many years in Dublin. Novelist and poet; his books of verse include *The Great Hunger* (1942), *Come Dance with Kitty Stobling* (1960), and *Collected Poems* (1964).

KIPLING, RUDYARD (1865–1936). British poet, novelist, and story writer, born in India, whose best-known works include "Gunga Din" and *Captains Courageous* (1897). Received the Nobel Prize for Literature in 1907.

LARKIN, MARY ANN (Born 1945). Poet and teacher, born in Pittsburgh of Irish-American parents, lives in Washington, D.C. Her published work includes *The Coil of the Skin* (1982).

LEWIS, C. DAY (1904–1972). British poet who also wrote criticism, detective novels (as Nicholas Blake), and books for children. Appointed Poet Laureate in 1968.

LONGLEY, MICHAEL (Born 1939). Born in Belfast. Poet, teacher, executive of Arts Council of Northern Ireland; books include *No Continuing City* (1969), *Man Lying on a Wall* (1976), and *Poems 1963–1983* (1985).

MCCARTHY, EUGENE (Born 1916). American writer and politician who represented Minnesota in the U.S. House of Representatives, 1949–58, and the U.S. Senate, 1958–70. Has published books of poetry, such as *Other Things and the Aardvark* (1970), as well as *Required Reading* (1981) and other collections of essays.

MACDONAGH, DONAGH (1912–1968). Son of Thomas MacDonagh, the Irish patriot and 1916 leader. District justice, broadcaster, playwright, and poet; books include *The Hungry Grass* (1947) and *A Warning to Conquerors* (1968).

MACNEICE, LOUIS (1907–1963). Born in Belfast, educated at Oxford, worked for the BBC for many years; wrote radio plays and numerous books of poetry, including *Autumn Journal* (1938), *Autumn Sequel* (1954), and *Visitations* (1957), with *Collected Poems* published posthumously (1966).

MAHON, DEREK (Born 1941). Born in Belfast. Poet, television writer, teacher, and lecturer; author of *Lives* (1972), *The Snow Party* (1975), *Poems 1962–1978* (1980), and *The Hunt by Night* (1983).

MANGAN, JAMES CLARENCE (1803–1849). Dublin writer who lived in poverty and died of cholera; most of his poetry was published posthumously, and a bronze bust was erected later in St. Stephen's Green, Dublin.

MARVELL, ANDREW (1621–1678). English poet best known for lyrics such as "The Garden," "To His Coy Mistress," and "Bermudas."

MATTHEWS, TOM (Born 1945). Brought up in Derry, lives in Larne, Co. Antrim, where he works as a chemist; his poetry has been published in *Dr. Wilson as an Arab* (1974).

MEYER, KUNO (1858–1919). German scholar and translator who played an important part in the revival of Irish literature.

MILTON, JOHN (1608–1674). English poet who supported the Puritan cause and Cromwell's government. Later in retirement he wrote his blank verse masterpieces, *Paradise Lost* (1667) and *Paradise Regained* (1671).

MONTAGUE, JOHN (Born 1929). Born in Brooklyn, New York; studied and taught at American universities; lived in Paris for many years; now lives in Ireland and teaches at University College, Cork. His poetry includes *Forms of Exile* (1958), *Patriotic Suite* (1966), *A Slow Dance* (1975), *The Dead Kingdom* (1984); he edited *The Faber Book of Irish Verse* (1974).

MOORE, MARIANNE (1887–1972). American poet, literary critic, and editor; awarded many honors, including both the Pulitzer Prize and the National Book Award in 1952.

MOORE, THOMAS (1779–1852). Dublin writer of songs and poems who became rich and famous through his series of *Irish Melodies* (1807–34). Largely responsible for the popularity of the harp and the shamrock as nationalistic symbols.

NÍ CHUILLEANAIN, EILEAN (Born 1942). Poet born in Cork, educated at Oxford and elsewhere. Books include *Site of Ambush* (1975), *Cork* (1977), *The Rose Geranium* (1981); she edited *Irish Women: Image and Achievement* (1985).

O'CONNOR, FRANK (NÉ MICHAEL O'DONOVAN) (1903–1966). Prolific writer, born in Cork, highly regarded for his short stories, starting with *Guests of the Nation* (1931). Also well known for his translations of Irish poetry in *Kings, Lords & Commons* (1959) and other books.

O'DONOVAN ROSSA, MARY (NÉE IRWIN) (1845–c. 1900). Poet, born in Clonakilty, Co. Cork; married the Irish patriot Jeremiah O'Donovan Rossa; published *Irish Lyrical Poems* (1868).

O'GRADY, DESMOND (Born 1935). Born in Limerick, educated at Harvard and elsewhere, lived in Paris and Rome, where he served as secretary to Ezra Pound. Poetry books include *Reilly* (1961), *The Dark Edge of Europe* (1967), *Sing Me Creation* (1977), and *A Limerick Rake* (1978).

O RAHILLY, EGAN (1670–1728). Kerry poet who lamented the destruction of the Irish aristocracy and its replacement by English planters and "upstarts."

ORMSBY, FRANK (Born 1947). Poet and teacher, born in Enniskillen, Co. Fermanagh; his work has been published in *A Store of Candles* (1977) and in *Poets from the North of Ireland* (1979), which he edited.

O'SHAUGHNESSY, ARTHUR (1844–1881). Poet who worked for many years at various jobs in the British Museum, London.

O'SULLIVAN, OWEN ROE (1748–1784). "The Red-haired" poet, itinerant farm laborer, occasional teacher; born and died tragically in Co. Kerry after many adventures in Ireland and elsewhere.

PARNELL, FANNY (1854–1883). Sister of Charles Stewart Parnell, very active in Irish politics; wrote for *The Nation* and served as secretary of the Ladies' Land League. Her poems have not been collected.

PAULIN, TOM (Born 1949). Poet and critic, born in Leeds, grew up in Belfast, educated at Oxford and elsewhere; poetry books include *A State of Justice* (1977), *The Strange Museum* (1980), and *Liberty Tree* (1983).

PAYNE, BASIL (Born 1928). Born in Dublin, widely traveled writer, translator, lecturer; his poetry books include *Sunlight on a Square* (1961), *Love in the Afternoon* (1966, 1971), and *Another Kind of Optimism* (1974).

PEARSE, PATRICK (1879–1916). Dublin writer, teacher, and patriot; an idealistic leader of the people, executed for his part in the Easter 1916 rising. *Collected Works* and other tributes published posthumously.

PROUT, FATHER (FRANCIS SYLVESTER MAHONY) (1804–1866). Born in Cork, died in Paris; Jesuit priest known for his learning and witty verses. He eventually left the Church and worked in Europe as journalist, translator, and satirist.

RODGERS, W. R. (1909–1969). Born in Belfast, died in Los Angeles. Minister, journalist, BBC producer and scriptwriter; his poetry books include *Europa and the Bull* (1952), *Ireland in Colour* (1956), and *Collected Poems* (1971).

ROLLESTON, T. W. (1857–1920). Poet, critic, and translator; born in Shinrone, died in Hampstead. Founder of *Dublin University Review* in 1885, first secretary of the Irish Literary Society in London; he edited the *Treasury of Irish Poetry* (1900) with Stopford Brooke.

RYAN, JOHN C. (Born c. 1960). Writer whose poems appear in *Riverine 2* and other Irish periodicals.

SIGERSON, DORA (1866–1918). Poet, born in Dublin, whose collections include *Sad Years* (1918).

SULLIVAN, CHARLES (Born 1933). Poet and educator, born in Boston of Irish-American parents; editor of illustrated books combining poetry and art, including *America in Poetry* (1988) and *Imaginary Gardens* (1989).

SWIFT, JONATHAN (1667–1745). Anglican priest, born in Ireland of English parents, became dean of St. Patrick's Cathedral, Dublin, in 1713. Fought for the rights of the poor, became famous as a satirist with *Gulliver's Travels* (1726). The "Stella" of his love poems, Esther Johnson, was a much younger woman who died in 1728, after which his health declined.

SYNGE, JOHN M. (1871–1909). Born and died in Dublin, but at the urging of Yeats he gathered material in the Aran Islands and other rural areas for plays to be produced at the Abbey Theatre, including *The Shadow of the Glen* (1903), *Riders to the Sea* (1904), and *The Playboy of the Western World* (1907). The realism of his work aroused loud and sometimes violent opposition from audiences more accustomed to sentimentality.

TODHUNTER, JOHN (1839–1916). Born in Dublin, studied medicine, became a doctor in 1871, but later gave up his practice and moved to London, where he devoted himself to writing plays and poetry, including *The Banshee* (1888) and *Three Irish Bardic Tales* (1896).

TWOMEY, CATHERINE (Born c. 1960). Poet whose work has been published in *Riverine 2* and other Irish periodicals.

TYNAN, KATHERINE (1861–1931). Born in Dublin, died in Wimbledon, England; a very prolific writer of prose and poetry, including *Shamrocks* (1887), *Irish Love Songs* (1892), *Flower of Youth* (1915), *The Holy War* (1926), and *Collected Poems* (1930).

WHITMAN, WALT (1819–1892). American poet and journalist whose interests were universal; his book *Leaves of Grass* (1855) was repeatedly revised and expanded.

WILDE, LADY JANE (1826–1896). Scholarly writer, born in Co. Wexford, who also published *Poems* (1864) under the pen name Speranza. Widowed in 1876, she moved to London, became impoverished, and died forgotten in the midst of her son Oscar's public disgrace.

YEATS, W. B. (1865–1939). Born in Dublin, died in France, but later reburied in Drumcliff churchyard, Co. Sligo. Achieved early fame with *Poems* (1895), *The Wind among the Reeds* (1899), *In the Seven Woods* (1903), and other volumes; awarded the Nobel Prize in 1923. Also served as a senator of the Irish Free State, 1922–28, and helped to found the Abbey Theatre, encouraging the work of John M. Synge and Sean O'Casey, among others.

YOUNG, AUGUSTUS (NÉ JAMES HOGAN) (Born 1943). Writer, born in Cork, lives in London; his publications include *Survival* (1969), *On Loaning Hill* (1970), and other books of poetry, as well as several translations and plays.

ACKNOWLEDGMENTS

Grateful acknowledgment is made for permission to reproduce the poems and illustrations in this book. All possible care has been taken to trace ownership of every selection and to make full acknowledgment (for illustrations, many sources are included in accompanying captions). If any errors or omissions have occurred, they will be corrected in subsequent editions, provided that notification is sent to the publisher.

POETRY

"Advent" by Patrick Kavanagh, from *Collected Poems*, The Gallery Press. Reprinted by kind permission of the estate of Patrick Kavanagh, ℅ Peter Fallon, Loughcrew, Oldcastle, Co. Meath, Ireland.

"Afterlives" (excerpt) by Derek Mahon. © Derek Mahon 1979. Reprinted from *Poems 1962–1978* by Derek Mahon (1979) by permission of Oxford University Press.

"Another Kind of Country" by Charles Sullivan. © 1988 Charles Sullivan.

"Antrim" by Robinson Jeffers. Copyright 1931 and renewed 1959 by Robinson Jeffers. Reprinted from *The Selected Poetry of Robinson Jeffers*, by permission of Random House, Inc.

"Are You Content?" by W. B. Yeats. Reprinted with permission of Macmillan Publishing Company from *Collected Poems* by W. B. Yeats. Copyright 1940 by Georgie Yeats, renewed 1968 by Bertha Georgie Yeats, Michael Butler Yeats, and Anne Yeats (U.S. rights). Reprinted by permission of A. P. Watt Limited on behalf of Michael B. Yeats and Macmillan London Ltd. (world rights).

"The Ballad of the Tinker's Wife" by Sigerson Clifford, from *Ballads of a Bogman*, published by The Mercier Press, 4, Bridge Street, Cork, Ireland.

"The Blackbird by Belfast Lough," trans. from the Irish by Frank O'Connor, from *Kings, Lords, & Commons*, Knopf. Reprinted by permission of Joan Daves. Copyright © 1959 Frank O'Connor; Copyright Renewed 1987 Harriet Sheehy.

"The Bomb Disposal" by Ciaran Carson is reprinted from *The New Estate* with the permission of Wake Forest University Press (U.S. rights). Reprinted with the permission of The Gallery Press, Loughcrew, Oldcastle, Co. Meath, Ireland, from *The New Estate and Other Poems* (1988) by Ciaran Carson (world rights).

"The Book of Kells" by Padraic Colum, The Dolmen Press. Reprinted with permission of the copyright holder, The Estate of Padraic Colum.

"Brightness of Brightness" by Egan O'Rahilly, trans. from the Irish by Frank O'Connor, from *Kings, Lords, & Commons*, Knopf. Reprinted by permission of Joan Daves. Copyright © 1959 Frank O'Connor; Copyright Renewed 1987 Harriet Sheehy.

"Cave" from "The Cave of Night" by John Montague is reprinted from *A Slow Dance* (1975) with the permission of Wake Forest University Press and Macmillan (N.Y.). Copyright John Montague.

"A Christmas Childhood" by Patrick Kavanagh, from *Collected Poems*, The Gallery Press. Reprinted by kind permission of the estate of Patrick Kavanagh, ℅ Peter Fallon, Loughcrew, Oldcastle, Co. Meath, Ireland.

"Cliona" by Catherine Twomey, from *Riverine 2* magazine, Winter/Spring 1988. Copyright 1988 by Catherine Twomey. Reprinted by permission of Edward Power, Editor, *Riverine 2* magazine.

"Company" by Michael Longley, from *Man Lying on a Wall*, Victor Gollancz, Ltd. Copyright Michael Longley.

"Coole Park, 1929" by W. B. Yeats. Reprinted with permission of Macmillan Publishing Company from *Collected Poems* by W. B. Yeats. Copyright 1933 by Macmillan Publishing Company, renewed 1961 by Bertha Georgie Yeats (U.S. rights). Reprinted by permission of A. P. Watt Limited on behalf of Michael B. Yeats and Macmillan London Ltd. (world rights).

"The Curse of Cromwell" by W. B. Yeats. Reprinted with permission of Macmillan Publishing Company from *Collected Poems* by W. B. Yeats. Copyright 1940 by Georgie Yeats, renewed 1968 by Bertha Georgie Yeats, Michael Butler Yeats, and Anne Yeats (U.S. rights). Reprinted by permission of A. P. Watt Limited on behalf of Michael B. Yeats and Macmillan London Ltd. (world rights).

"The Dance Half Done" by Mary Ann Larkin, from *The Coil of the Skin*. Copyright Mary Ann Larkin.

"A Day in August" by Frank Ormsby, from *A Store of Candles*, Oxford University Press. Reprinted from *A Store of Candles*, © 1977, 1986, by kind permission of the author and The Gallery Press, Loughcrew, Oldcastle, Co. Meath, Ireland.

"Death of an Irishwoman" by Michael Hartnett, from *Poems in English*. Copyright © Michael Hartnett and reprinted with the permission of Michael Hartnett.

"Derry" by Seamus Deane, from *Gradual Wars*, Irish Academic Press. Copyright 1973 by Seamus Deane. Permission to reprint by Seamus Deane.

"Derry Morning" by Derek Mahon. © Derek Mahon 1982. Reprinted from *The Hunt by Night* by Derek Mahon (1982) by permission of Oxford University Press.

"Digging" by Seamus Heaney, from *Poems 1965–1975* by Seamus Heaney. Copyright © 1966, 1969, 1972, 1975, 1980 by Seamus Heaney. Reprinted by permission of Farrar, Straus and Giroux, Inc. (U.S. rights). Reprinted by permission of Faber and Faber Limited from *Death of a Naturalist* by Seamus Heaney (world rights).

"Docker" by Seamus Heaney, from *Poems 1965–1975* by Seamus Heaney. Copyright © 1966, 1969, 1972, 1975, 1980 by Seamus Heaney. Reprinted by permission of Farrar, Straus and Giroux, Inc. (U.S. rights). Reprinted by permission of Faber and Faber Limited from *Death of a Naturalist* by Seamus Heaney (world rights).

"Dowager" by John Montague is reprinted from *A Slow Dance* (1984) with the permission of Wake Forest University Press and Macmillan (N.Y.). Copyright John Montague.

"The Downfall of Heathendom," trans. from the Irish by Frank O'Connor, from *Kings, Lords, & Commons*, Knopf. Reprinted by permission of Joan Daves. Copyright © 1959 Frank O'Connor; Copyright Renewed 1987 Harriet Sheehy.

"Dublin" by Louis MacNeice, reprinted by permission of Faber and Faber Limited from *The Collected Poems of Louis MacNeice*.

"Easter 1916" by W. B. Yeats. Reprinted with permission of Macmillan Publishing Company from *Collected Poems* by W. B. Yeats. Copyright 1924 by Macmillan Publishing Company, renewed 1952 by Bertha Georgie Yeats (U.S. rights). Reprinted by permission of A. P. Watt Limited on behalf of Michael B. Yeats and Macmillan London Ltd. (world rights).

"Enemy Encounter" by Padraic Fiacc (Patrick Joseph O'Connor), from *Poets from the North of Ireland*, by permission of The Blackstaff Press.

"Field Day" by W. R. Rodgers, from *Collected Poems*, Oxford University Press. © W. R. Rodgers 1971. Reprinted by permission of Mrs. Lucy Rodgers Cohen.

"Follower" by Seamus Heaney, from *Poems 1965–1975* by Seamus Heaney. Copyright © 1966, 1969, 1972, 1975, 1980 by Farrar, Straus and Giroux, Inc. (U.S. rights). Reprinted by permission of Faber and Faber Limited from *Death of a Naturalist* by Seamus Heaney (world rights).

"For My Grandmother, Bridget Halpin" by Michael Hartnett, from *Selected Poems*. Copyright © Michael Hartnett and reprinted with the permission of Michael Hartnett.

"For Paddy Mac" by Padraic Fallon, from *Poems*, The Dolmen Press. Reprinted with the permission of the estate of Padraic Fallon.

"The Gardener" from "Novelettes III" (excerpt) by Louis MacNeice,

ILLUSTRATIONS